Piero
former Superintendent of A
for the Provinces of

Siena

New practical guide

Contrade and Palio
150 color photos
Useful information
Plan of the town

BONECHI EDIZIONI "IL TURISMO"

© Copyright by Bonechi Edizioni "Il Turismo" S.r.l.
Via G. Di Vittorio, 31 - 50145 FLORENCE
Tel. +39 055.37.57.39
Fax +39 055.37.47.01
e-mail: bbonechi@dada.it
        info@bonechionline.com
http://www.bonechionline.com
All rights reserved
Printed in Italy

Photos: Bonechi Edizioni "Il Turismo" S.r.l. and Fabio Lensini (Siena) Archives
Photos pages: 99-100: Courtesy of the Ministry for Cultural Assets and Affairs - State Archives of Siena - auth. nr. 354 dated 17.12.98
Photos pages 28-29-30: by permission of the Banca Monte dei Paschi di Siena, authorization dated 04.12.98
Layout: Lorenzo Gualtieri
Cover: Paola Rufino
Maps: Lorenzo Cerrina
Editing: Lorena Lazzari
Photolithography: La Nuova Lito S.n.c., Florence

ISBN 978-88-7204-379-0

* *The book presents the locations of the artworks at the time of printing*

Siena was founded by the Romans during the reign of Octavian Augustus. They built a military colony (Saena Julia) on the site of a preexisting Etruscan and perhaps Gallic (the Saenones) settlement. The Roman origins of the town explain the heraldic charge the Medieval town chose for itself (the She-wolf feeding Romulus and Remus), which, together with the argent and sable coat divided per fess (la Balzana) were used by the town as its arms. Roman Siena was never very important, chiefly because it did not lie on any of the main consular roads (Aurelia and Cassia), which originally wound along the coast and through the Chiana Valley. For the same reasons, Chris-

tianity only reached Sienese territory towards the beginning of the IV century. After the first Barbarian invasions had swept through Italy and after the Byzantine-Gothic war, Siena became part of the Lombard dominions. The Lombards settled in Siena and promoted the expansion of the Sienese territory to the detriment of nearby Arezzo. The road network shifted its axis and the Aurelia and the Cassia, which passed through areas exposed to the Byzantine raids, were gradually abandoned in favor of the Via Francigena, that linked the Northern Lombard possessions with Rome, passing through Siena. In 774, the Lombards surrendered to Charlemagne and Siena was overrun by Frankish adminis-

View of Siena.

trators, who married into the Lombard families, originating the oldest aristocratic families in Siena and founding abbeys and castles all over the Sienese territory. Feudal power gradually decreased and at the death of the Countess Matilda (1115), the Mark of Tuscia, which under the Canossa family (Matilda's) included most of Tuscany as it is today, broke up into a series of fledgling communal structures. The Commune of Siena, with its territory bordering dangerously on Guelph Florence, a traditional enemy of Siena, declared its allegiance to the Ghibelline cause. Between the XII and XIII centuries, the early-Medieval «civitas» of Siena expanded, joining the two boroughs or agglomerations of houses that had grown up along the Via Francigena, to the north and east of the town, thus originating the three districts, *terzi*, of Città, Camollia and San Martino. Money-lending and exchange activities brought the city great prosperity, the business expanded all over Europe (Champagne, Flanders and England) and under the Buonsignori created the largest European banking company in the XIII century. The large Sienese hospital of S. Maria della Scala that had been founded by the cathedral canons prior to the year one thousand also gained in importance during this period, and the office of the Biccherna (the financial magistrature) and the General Council became stronger as well. Towards the beginning of the XIII century, the consular regime was replaced by the Podestà system and Siena became one of the most active Tuscan partisans of Frederick II's successor, Manfred of Swabia, King of Sicily. The war against Florence reached its apex at the battle of Montaperti,

View of Siena.

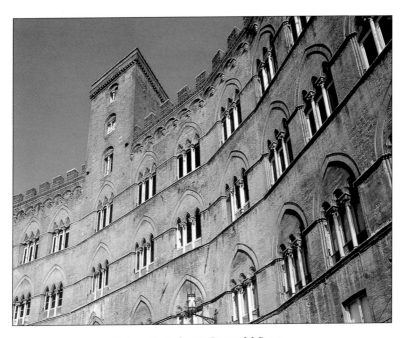

Palazzo Sansedoni in Piazza del Campo.

when the Sienese army massacred the Guelph army of Florence (4 September 1260). The regime of the Podestàs fell in Siena as it did in the Northern and Central Italian towns, when the burgher class started demanding that it should share the administrative power in the town together with the patricians. The regime of the Nine commenced in 1287 and lasted for many tranquil years. Its representatives were mostly rich burghers who were appointed in rotation every two months. This was the period during which the Salimbeni, Tolomei, Sansedoni, Buonsignori, Piccolomini and Gallerani families rose to power and countless great artists such as Duccio di Buoninsegna, Simone Martini, Ambrogio and Piero Lorenzetti, Nicola and Giovanni Pisano, Tino da Ca-

maino and many others graced Siena with their presence. These were the years when the construction of the Palazzo Pubblico was commenced, when the plans for enlarging the Cathedral (never completed) were drawn, when the last circle of the walls (still standing) was built. In 1348, Siena, like most of Europe, was hit by the terrible Black Death, which not only exterminated four fifths of the population, but destabilized the political scene. When the Government of the Nine was overthrown, in 1355, the "Monti" or groups of powerful patrician and burgher families took over the government. Caterina Benincasa (St. Catherine of Siena), a typical exponent of Medieval religious Siena, lived during this period, and Bartolo di Fredi, Taddeo di Bartolo, An-

5

drea di Bartolo, etc. emerged on the painting scene. During the 1390's, in order to protect herself from Florence, Siena placed herself under the Seigneury of Gian Galeazzo Visconti, Duke of Milan, but after his death (1404), the turbulent, communal strife resumed. These were the years in which the great Sienese painters flourished such as Sassetta, Vecchietta, Francesco di Giorgio Martini, and Sano di Pietro. The outstanding sculptor of the period was Jacopo della Quercia, while the humanist pope Pius II (Enea Silvio Piccolomini) promoted the activity on Sienese soil of Florentine artists like Bernardo Rossellino. At the end of the fifteenth century Siena had to accept the alliance with Charles V of Spain, who ordered a fortress built for the Spanish forces within the town, arousing violent popular reaction that led to the break-up of the alliance (1552) with the Emperor of Spain, who then sought the support of Cosimo I de'Medici in Florence. Siena became an ally of France, but in the end, beleaguered by the Florentine and Spanish forces, was forced to capitulate in April 1555. Siena was handed over to Philip II, King of Spain who granted it in fief to Cosimo

The Palazzo Pubblico in a XIX century engraving.

I de'Medici (who thus became Duke of Florence and Siena and subsequently, in 1569, Grand Duke of Tuscany, thanks to the extension of the territories under his power). Under the Medici family, Siena clung to the memory of her former freedom and the factious spirit of her inhabitants, no longer allowed to participate in the political life of the city, was unleashed in passionate allegiance to the respective «contrade» of each native of Siena. The city maintained its independence in the artistic field, thanks to Domenico Beccafumi, Baldassarre Peruzzi and others. The banking tradition evolved from the private to the public status and the ancient Monte di Pietà, founded in 1472 became the Monte dei Paschi in 1624. After the advent of the Hapsburg-Lorraine family (1737), the last vestiges of the Republic disappeared and the city became an integral part of the Grand Duchy of Tuscany. The city's marked spiritual individuality is however apparent today in the attachment each Sienese feels towards his or her contrada and in the passionate involvement in the Palio, the most evident example of the exuberant nature of Siena's citizens.

Piazza del Campo seen from the Mangia Tower.

Over the centuries, the different styles which have grown into each other in the various patrician mansions arranged around the Piazza del Campo have produced an overall harmony, making it one of the most fascinating main squares in Europe. The middle of the square is paved with handmade bricks, laid in a herringbone pattern, and divided by nine strips of travertine in honor of the Government of the Nine Lords (i Signori Nove) that presided over the town from 1285 to 1355. Nearly all the important events in Siena's history have taken place in or around this square. Some of them were auspicious, others less so; some took place during the glorious era of the Re-

Piazza del Campo.

7

1. Palazzo Petroni
2. Palazzo Piccolomini Salamoneschi
3. Palazzo Piccolomini
4. Palazzo Ragnoni
5. Palazzo Mezolombardi-Rinaldini
6. Palazzo Tornainpuglia Sansedoni
7. Palazzo Vincenti
8. Palazzo Piccolomini
9. Palazzo Rimbotti (formerly R. Angioleri)
10. Sede della Mercanzia
11. Palazzo Saracini
12. Palazzo Scotti
13. Palazzo Accarigi
14. Palazzo Alessi
15. Palazzo Mattasala Lambertini
16. The Beringieri-Antolini House

public (before 1555), others after the city became a dominion of Florence. It was period of domination that was never fully accepted by that intense spirit of republican freedom that is still an example for today's democracies. Of all the events in the square, most important was and still is the Palio horse race. It is held here every year on 2 July and on 16 August. It is impossible to speak of the history of Siena and her people without mentioning the "contrade" and the Palio. The race is not a mere popular tradition or folkloristic event, but a true synthesis of an ancient custom of a people who, throughout the year, in every important public or private act or deed relives and merges past and present in a remarkable continuity, as in a small but real democratic republic.

In order to channel water from distant Staggia to Piazza del Campo, Giacomo di Vanni di Ugolino (later called Giacomo dell'Acqua) spent about eight years digging great underground canals (which are still known as the Bottini) which, as they approached the town precincts, widened into brick-lined galleries of exceptional technical and artistic interest. Charles V, after visiting the Sienese "bottini", is supposed to have exclaimed that Siena was two cities in one, each as beautiful as the other, the first underground, the second above. Water was conveyed to Piazza del Campo through a master-conduit, most likely first utilized around 1342. "The Sienese saluted the event with great rejoicing", wherefore the fountain, appropriately named Fonte Gaia (Joyous Fountain), was built the following year (1343). The XIV century Fonte Gaia, about which we have practically no information, was replaced in 1419 by Jacopo della Quercia's and then by Tito Sarrocchi's free adaptation of it in 1858. The two statues of Rhea Silvia and Acca Larentis, that Jacopo had placed at each end of his fountain, were omitted from Sarrocchi's copy. The original sculptures by Jacopo della Quercia are now in a room in the old Ospedale di S. Maria della Scala that overlooks Piazza Duomo. Although its present state is decidedly lamentable, Jacopo's Fonte Gaia is still one of the most important sculptures produced in XV century Italy during the transition from the Gothic to the Renaissance styles. The *Madonna*

and Child, a symbol taken from Lorenzetti's Allegory of Good Government, is flanked by two angels, the *Theological* and *Cardinal Virtues* and by *Justice*. Successive changes in the project led Jacopo to add the statues of the *Expulsion from Paradise*, the *Creation of Adam* as well as the two statues of *Acca Larentis* and *Rhea Silvia* (respectively mother and nurse of Romulus and Remus, symbolizing Charity and Liberality). These were the first two statues of female nudes to stand in a public place, who were neither Eve nor a repentant saint.

Jacopo della Quercia, detail; above, *the Gaia Fountain today.*

9

Because of a solemn vow made during the terrible plague of 1348, the Commune of Siena commissioned the Cappella di Piazza which stands out at the foot of the Mangia Tower. At first, Domenico di Agostino, then master builder at the Opera del Duomo (Cathedral Works) and brother to the better known Giovanni, was put in charge of the project. The four corner piers, called "more", were built somewhat later, in 1376 by Giovanni di Cecco.

Chapel of Piazza del Campo.

A plain roof covered the piers until Antonio Federighi replaced it during the Renaissance (1461-1468) with a vaulted roof, supported by rounded arches, with niches in the corners, garlands adorning the pendentives and a purely classical architrave decorated with a frieze of gryphons and vases. The side balustrades are two XIII century marble panels, which are thought to have come from the ancient Baptismal Font in the Cathedral. The two figures of Arithmetic and Geometry, on the front panels, were sculpted by Guidoccio Cozzarelli (1470). In 1848, they were replaced by copies carved by Enea Becheroni while the Cozzarelli originals were placed inside the Palace on the walls of the main staircase. The elegant grilles in wrought iron on either side of the Chapel were made in the second half of the XIV century. They probably belonged to the first Chapel of the Nine, on the ground floor of the Palazzo Pubblico, and were forged by Pietro di Betto, helped, according to some accounts, by Conte di Lello Orlandi, another Sienese master smith. To the left of the altar, behind a small, old wrought iron grille, there is a stone shrine, with an *Annunciation* and a *Christ Blessing* on the tympanum, by an unknown Sienese carver of the late XIV century. The figures are reminiscent of Goro di Gregorio's style. The fresco above the altar, with the *Madonna and Child, Angels and the Almighty*, is almost indecipherable. It was painted by Sodoma between 1537 and 1539.

It is thought that the first nucleus was a low, one-story construction with a simple stone façade, and four openings leading into a large hall and a courtyard, that was finished around 1284 as related by the chronicles of Paolo Tommaso Montauri that year. In 1288, however, the Council decided to construct a new palace at the bottom of the Campo. A few years later, the construction of the central part of the palace was commenced. It was not unlike the building we see today: the stone-dressed ground-floor with its four ogival openings; the first brick story with four triple mullioned windows and the second story, also in brick, which probably had five triple mullioned windows to start with, but later reduced to four, for the sake of uniformity, while the two second floor wings were added in 1680, in the Baroque period. The building was probably finished around 1310, as the Government of the Nine adopted it as their headquarters in that year. The nine members of the government were never allowed out of the palace except on Feast days. The ground-floor façade had ten open doorways, of which the fourth from the right of anyone looking at the building, led into the Chapel of the Nine, frescoed by XIV century painters. After the fairly drastic restoration carried out during the late 1890s and the early 1900s, the façade has taken on a plain, fairly undecorated appearance. The architectural elements soar vertically upwards, only

A bird's eye view of Siena.

11

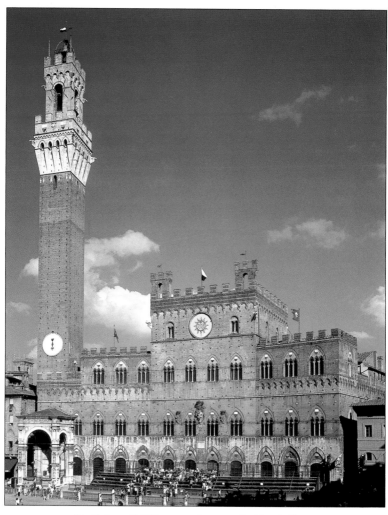

The Palazzo Pubblico; opposite page: *the Mangia Tower.*

interrupted by the large double and triple mullioned windows and countering all sense of massive strength with the frail elegance of the façade's delicate linearism. The Siena *arms* or *Balzana* are set into the ogival arch of each window, whilst the great *Plaque of St. Bernardino* (the monogram of Christ, IHS, surrounded by rays) replaces the orig-inal central twin mullioned window on the third story level. The *Medici arms* were added in 1560 to commemorate the annexation of Siena to the Grand Duchy of Tuscany. The Medici crest is flanked by the *Balzana* and by the people's *Lion Rampant.* Two stone *she-wolf* gargoyles protrude on each side of the central block. The main entrance tympanum has the *Lion of the people* in the center, flanked by two She-wolves in relief while a statuette of *St. Ansanus* stands above the tympanum. At the end of the façade, near the main entrance, there used to be a granite column bearing the gilded bronze *she-wolf with the Roman twins*, cast by Giovanni and Lorenzo di Turino in 1430. This beautiful group has now been placed inside the palace in order to preserve it. The she-wolf suckling Romulus and Remus is the symbol of Siena. The mythical brothers, Aschius and Senius, sons of Remus, are supposed to have fled from the wrath of Romulus, bearing an effigy of the Roman She-wolf, as a symbol of their lost homeland, with them. They reputedly took refuge in the Tuscan hills, where Senius later founded the city (Senius/ Sena/Siena).

The **Mangia Tower**, which gets its name from Giovanni di Balduccio or Duccio, who was nicknamed Mangiaguadagni (literally earnings-gobbler) or Mangia (Gobbler), who used to be the bell-ringer before a mechanism was installed to replace him, lends the whole complex of the Palazzo Pubblico its extraordinarily delicate, vertical elegance. It was started in 1325 and finished in 1348. It was intended as a symbol of the power residing in the palace and of the city itself. The tower is 87 m. high (102 m., if we include the lightening rod). The brothers Francesco and Muccio (or Minuccio) di Rinaldo from Arezzo were commissioned to do the construction work (1338-40) and they therefore shouldered the risks and expense of the building operations The tower is entirely in brick, up to the soaring white travertine pronged supports of the belfry balustrade, which give the whole tower the appearance of a tall slender lily. The latter part was probably built by Agostino di Giovanni, based on the designs of a certain "Master Lippo-painter", almost certainly the great Lippo Memmi, brother-in-law to Simone Martini (1341). The present master bell (called "Campanone", or "Sunto") weighs 6764 kgs. and was hung in the belfry in 1666.

There are, at present two entries to the Town Hall on the Piazza. The first,

The Mangia Tower and the Courtyard of the Podestà;
below: *the Loggia on the top floor of the palace.*

through the two doors to the left, next to the Chapel, leads into the **Courtyard of the Podestà** where, amidst the many *family crests* of the governors, the remains of the stone *statue of Mangia* are preserved. At the end of the courtyard, steps lead up to the **Teatro dei Rinnovati**, formerly the Great Council Chamber of the Republic. A side door opens onto a modern staircase leading down to a whole series of lovely, semi-underground halls, with brick vaults, once the cisterns and store-rooms of the Palace ("**Magazzini del Sale**" or "Salt Storerooms"), which have been beautifully restored and are now used for temporary exhibitions. The same staircase leads to the piano nobile and the rooms containing the **Quadreria** or Picture Gallery of various schools and periods, mostly moved here from the old Civic Museum. The next room is the **Room of the Risorgimento** (the former Audience Room of the Podestà) where a large number of XIX century sculptures have been arranged. The Room of the Risorgimento, however, is known for the scenes on the walls, by XIX century Tuscan artists, recounting episodes from the life of Vittorio Emanuele II.

The other door, on the right, opens onto a corridor, leading to a steep staircase, which climbs up to the Loggia and the upper floors. Beyond

Sala di Balia.

the corridor one enters the **Sala di Balia** (Hall of the Aldermen), where the Bailie (the representatives of the executive power of the Republic, generally eight citizens, with extensive powers), met from 1455 on. The hall is completely frescoed in Late Gothic style by a Sienese (Martino di Bartolomeo) and by a citizen of Arezzo, who had learned his craft in Florence Spinello Aretino, who was, in fact, named after his hometown). The former painted the *Virtues* on the vault sections and on the pillars and the f*our Evangelists* on the intrados of the great arch that divides the hall into two, as well as six *busts of emperors and warriors*, including, they say, Godfrey of Bouillon, on the piers and pendentives of the arch itself. In 1408, Spinello Aretino was given the more complicated task of recording the *deeds of Pope Alexander III*, a

Sala di Balia: detail of a fresco
by Spinello Aretino;
below: ***the Inner Chapel***

The Inner Chapel: the Funeral of
the Virgin, by Taddeo di Bartolo;
right: Inlay by Domenico di Niccolò.

member of the Sienese Bandinelli
family, the inspiring force behind
the Lombard League and deadly
enemy of Barbarossa (Frederick
Redbeard) as well as probable pro-
moter of the foundation of the Cathedral of Siena.

The beautiful inlaid *door*, (1426)
which leads into the **Inner Chapel**,
is attributed to Domenico di Niccolò (called «dei Cori» because he
also made the wonderful carved
and inlaid *choir stalls* of the palace
chapel). The magnificent choir flanking the altar was carved by
Domenico di Niccolò between 1514
and 1428. There are 21 stalls each
decorated with a scene illustrating
some article of the Creed. Also by
Domenico, the splendid left door
frame decorated with a Nativity
scene and a *Wheel*, symbolizing the

allegories of good and bad power.
The vaults and walls of the chapel
were all frescoed by the late-Gothic
Sienese painter, Taddeo di Bartolo,
with five *Scenes from the Life of the
Virgin.* On the altar there is painting by Antonio Bazzi who was
known as Sodoma, portraying the
Holy Family and *St. Leonard*; this
is one of the most significant paintings by the artist from Vercelli who
belonged to Leonardo's school
(1530-35). There is a carved and
gilded wooden *chandelier* hanging

from the vault of the chapel; it had incorrectly been attributed to Cecco di Nanni del Ciucca and painted by Cristofano da Cosona. It has more recently been recognized as having been carved by Domenico di Niccolò dei Cori shortly before 1435. Taddeo di Bartolo also painted the colossal *St. Christopher* (1408) and a cycle of political Virtues and illustrious men (1414) in the **Antechapel**; the cycle quite obviously refers to the ideas and lifestyle of the Sienese republic in the early XV century. There are five *Virtues* illustrated (*Fortitude, Prudence, Faith, Justice and Magnanimity*), surrounded by the portraits of illustrious personalities of ancient Rome (*Cato, Brutus, Mutius Scaevola, Attilius Reg-*

The Map Room;
below: *the Inner Chapel, the Holy Family by Sodoma.*

ulus, Scipio, etc.). The intrados of the great arch, on the Sala del Mappamondo (Map Room) side, is decorated with a *view of Rome,* surrounded by the figures of *Jupiter, Mars, Apollo, Pallas Athena, Aristotle, Caesar and Pompey.* In 1959, the gilded bronze She-wolf, feeding the twins was placed in the vestibule. The statue was cast in 1429 by Giovanni di Turino and his son Lorenzo and was placed on the column in front of the Palazzo Pubblico.

Next to the chapel is the great hall, called **Sala del Mappamondo** (Map Room), where the Council of the Republic met. The end wall is decorated by Simone Martini's magnificent **Maestà** (1315 and 1321), one of the greatest European Gothic masterpieces. The novel significant concepts this work expresses, com-

The Map Room;
Maestà by Simone Martini and a detail.

pared for instance, with the other famous *Maestà* by Duccio di Buoninsegna in the Museo dell'Opera del Duomo (Cathedral Museum) are a perfect definition of the new ideals of the XIV century, which blossom in the pages of Petrarch's Canzoniere (Petrarch was a friend of Simone) or in Boccacio's Decameron. Simone's frescoed Virgin no longer conforms to the strict canons of Byzantine iconography, as Duccio's Madonna does in his gigantic panel. She is a more human «Mater», who has graciously descended amidst the people of Siena, while two angels offer bowls brimming with flowers, as she sits among her heavenly retinue. These were new emotions compared with the early Middle Ages. It is the compositional aspect that is more revolutionary than the figures and the subject, with harmonious lines flowing almost uninterruptedly from one figure to the other, and soft, transparent colors. The upper part of the end wall opposite the Maestà is frescoed with the *1328 Siege of the Castle of Montemassi in Maremma led by Guido Riccio da Fogliano*, then captain of the Sienese army. Simone Martini's name is also linked to this world-famous fresco that has become the symbol of the civilian and military glory of the ancient Republic of

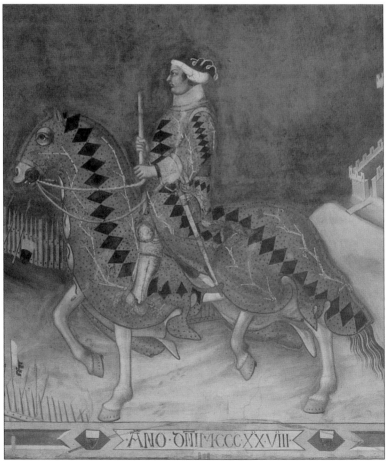

The Map Room: The Siege of the Castle of Montemassi, by Simone Martini.

Although the features of the knight are portrayed with due attention, the central group appears to possess no physical solidity whatsoever, as if the modulated construction were an abstract symphony of pure musical chords, repeated in the flowing fine of lozenges on the caparisoned horse and on the knight's tunic, the whole offset by the unstable equilibrium of the horse, that seems to be floating in mid-air. This unreal metaphysical quality enhances the magic of the scene. Its apparition-like sense can also be perceived in the landscape, where the castle of Montemassi, the keep with its turrets and catapult and the Sienese army encampment stand out against the barren clay hills of the Maremma. During careful restorations in 1981, under the direction of this writer, yet another exceptional fresco was

Siena and is a kind of contrast to the religious glory epitomized by the courtly language used in the Maestà on the opposite wall. The knight in his tunic embroidered with the device of the Da Fogliano family (twining vines sprouting from a line of dark blue lozenges on golden ground) rides a horse caparisoned with the same device.

The Map Room: The Surrender of a Castle, (Duccio di Buonisegna?).

On these pages: *The Room of Peace: Good Government in the City of Siena,*
by Ambrogio Lorenzetti.

found below the Guidoriccio scene. It is certainly older and depicts the *peaceful surrender of a castle* (Giuncarico in Maremma) to the Sienese. This fresco can most probably be attributed to Duccio di Buoninsegna (1314-1315). Adjacent to the Map Room is the Room of the Nine, bet-

The Room of Peace: Allegory of Good Government, by Ambrogio Lorenzetti.

ter known as the **Room of Peace**, thanks to an allegorical figure painted there. The frescoes, of great artistic and historic value, are world-famous. They cover three sides of the room and represent the *Allegory of Good and Bad Government*, which the great Ambrogio Lorenzetti was commissioned to paint for the Government of the Nine, between 1338 and 1340. On the short wall opposite the large windows is the Allegory of Good Government proper. It is rich in inscriptions identifying the various figures and centers on the old man, dressed in black and white (the colors of Siena) symbolizing both the city and the common weal; the she-wolf feeding the twins is at his feet. The old man is flanked by *Peace, Fortitude, Prudence, Magnanimity, Temperance* and *Justice*, with *Faith, Hope* and *Charity* above his head. Knights in armor stand guard, below right, over a group of prisoners or evil-doers. The slow procession of the rulers conversing among themselves winds its way towards him, while the knights and prisoners add a note of deeper humanity to the magnificent composition. The ethical and political meanings which Simone Martini expressed in a totally different vein in the frescoes we have just described in the Map Room, are reiterated in this Allegory by Ambrogio in a far more precise and less abstract fashion with the object of pointing out that a good government can only be based on the Virtues (with special reference to Justice and Concord) which spontaneously generate Safety, flying high above the red gate of Siena, in the fresco on the right wall. Ambrogio's cycle (the first to be

The Room of the Concistory;
below: *The Judgment of Solomon,
by Luca Giordano.*

ment on Siena and its territory. The delightfully realistic details of the happy, well-governed city, inhabited by its content, industrious citizens engaged in their manifold activities both within and outside the walls are depicted in all their variety beneath the winged figure of Safety hovering above the russet gate of Siena. This is the first painting in the history of art that timeless modernity is expressed without the mediation of symbolism: a happy life is depicted in the city and countryside, with shops open on the street, a school, pro-

based on a secular theme in the history of painting, as many critics have observed) reaches its peak on the right wall, where he portrayed the *Effects of Good Govern-* cessions, and children playing. The contentment of the farmers harvesting their crops, and the beautiful countryside are portrayed through masterful use of color. On the opposite wall, much of the fresco of the effects of *Bad Government* has been destroyed over the years due to carelessness. The allegory itself centers on the figure of *Tyranny* enthroned. At his feet is a black Billy-goat (*Bestiality*) and he is flanked by the sinister figures of *Cruelty, Deceit, Fraudulence, Fury, Discord* and *War. Avarice, Pride* and *Vainglory* crowd around his head. The humiliated figure of Justice in chains crouches beneath the throne. After admiring other, minor works in the last room, we retrace our steps through the antechapel and enter the last room via an elegant Renaissance marble doorway, carved by Bernardo Rossellino in 1446, (the carved and inlaid doors were made by Domenico di Niccolò dei Cori in 1444). The hall is called **Sala del Concistoro** (Room of the Concistory), or Room of the Tapestries, because of the three magnificent Gobelin tapestries, woven to designs by Charles Le Brun (XVII century) hanging on the walls. They

*Detail of a fresco
by Sano di Pietro
in the ground floor hall.*

represent the *Allegories of Earth, Air* and *Fire*. The fourth, with the Allegory of Water is still in the Uffizi gallery in Florence, where the three Sienese ones originally came from.

The great artistic importance of this room, is mainly due, however, to the superbly luminous frescoes that Domenico di Pace, called Beccafumi, painted between 1529 and 1535 on the ceiling vaults. Like Ambrogio Lorenzetti before him, in the Room of Peace, he depicted episodes of *civic Virtue* drawn from Valerius Maximus. Beccafumi's brilliant colors create a sensation of crystalline purity and transparent delicacy and the clarity of the fresco's luminous tones, combined with the airy, beautifully executed perspective are in perfect accord with the most refined Tuscan Mannerist dictates, to such an extent that the technical and pictorial ability employed lend the whole a vaguely cold and artificial sensation. There is an admirable painting by Luca Giordano (Naples 1634-1705) of the *Judgement of Solomon* above the doorway. The robust chiaroscuro effects owe much to another Neapolitan painter Mattia Preti, but also reflect a resounding range of chromatic effects drawn from the neo-Venetian school. It was probably painted around 1675-80, before Giordano left for Florence. Today, most of the offices of the city government

The Room of the Concistory: The Murder of Spurio Melio, by Beccafumi.

are on the ground-floor of the palace and can be entered from Piazza del Campo via the second door on the right. Many of the ground floor rooms are also decorated with paintings and mainly frescoes, by more or less renowned artists starting from the XIV century, followers of Simone Martini, Bartolo di Fredi, Sano di Pietro, Vecchietta, Sodoma, Rutilio Manetti, and other XVIII century Sienese painters.

In the XIV century, splendid family mansions, nearly all in brick with double or triple-mullioned windows surrounded the square, as a decree contained in the Statute of the Republic ordained. They were separated by the narrow alleys leading into the square itself. The diagram on page 8 shows who owned each mansion in the Middle Ages. Even though most of these buildings were transformed or even entirely rebuilt, the original harmony of the Medieval square is still evident.

From Piazza del Campo, we must go up the *Costarella dei Barbieri* to reach the Cathedral. This is starting point and finish line for the Palio race. Opposite, on Via di Città, is the tower-house that used to be the seat of the Podestà (governor) of Siena, which leads on to the *neighboring Palazzo Pollini*, that stands between the left corner of the Costarella and the Via di Città, which, at this point starts ascending slowly towards the old city center. *Via di Città*, formerly Via Galgaria, is one of the loveliest and most elegant streets in Siena. It is lined with buildings constructed in various periods, starting from the XIII century, when many wooden houses were replaced by stone and brick structures.

PALAZZO CHIGI-SARACINI

Further on, on the left, at number 89, stands Palazzo Chigi Saracini, a stone building decorated in brick. In the XIII century, the original nucleus of the house belonged to the Marescotti family, who throughout the XIV century gradually incorporated the neighboring buildings, and, in much the same way as other powerful families of Siena, erected a kind of great, fortified town residence, called the «Castellare». The typically Sienese Gothic architectural elements are mostly XIV century, but there are several Renaissance additions as well. In 1781, Galgano Saracini enlarged the façade, conforming the whole to the older part. The build-

Palazzo Chigi-Saracini;
below: ***Epiphany by Stefano di Giovanni, known as Sassetta** (Chigi-Saracini Collection, property of the Monte dei Paschi di Siena).*

ing was last restored by the painter, architect and sculptor Arturo Vigliardi in 1923 who dedicated much attention to the concert hall. He created a definitely XVIII century atmosphere, and even painted a great fresco on the ceiling vault, in the style of Tiepolo, depicting *the Triumphant Return of the Sienese Army after the Battle of Montaperti.* The two modern bronzes that represent Harmony and Melody are by the Sienese sculptor Fulvio Corsini. The transformation was commissioned by Count Guido Saracini, last of his line, so that the famous **Accademia Musicale Chigiana** (Chigiana Musical Academy) could have a larger concert hall. The Academy was founded by Count Guido (who died in 1965) and has now become an officially recognized corporate body chaired by the President of the Monte dei Paschi di Siena bank, which partially funds it. The Academy is considered one of the most prestigious in the world, not only because of the high quality of the concerts it presents (the Settimana Musicale Chigiana is a well-known festival), but also because of the hundreds of young musicians who flock to Siena every year from all over the world in order to attend the master classes held in Palazzo Chigi Saracini by the most

The Concert Hall;
above: *Ceramic plate, Manifattura S. Quirico d'Orcia*
(Chigi-Saracini Collection, property of the Monte dei Paschi di Siena).

The Scarlatti or Beccafumi room; above: ***David and Bathsheba by Bernardino Mei (Chigi-Saracini Collection, property of the Monte dei Paschi di Siena).***

renowned musicians of our time. Thanks chiefly to the generosity of Galgano Saracini, Palazzo Chigi Saracini also contains a large and exceptionally interesting collection of Sienese paintings ranging from the 13th to the XVIII century (Sassetta, Sano di Pietro, Beccafumi, Sodoma, etc.). The many rooms of the mansion are furnished and decorated with hundreds of *paintings, sculptures, furniture, objects d'art, porcelain,* archeological finds (*Etruscan urns, bucchero, vases* etc.), valuable *musical instruments,* and more.

FROM THE CAMPO TO THE CATHEDRAL

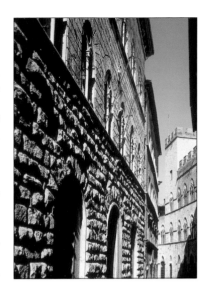

Just beyond Palazzo Chigi Saracini, on the right, we see the imposing **Palazzo Piccolomini**, called *Palazzo delle Papesse*, one of the most perfect examples of Florentine Renaissance architecture, probably built to plans by Rossellino (1460-95) and currently the head quarters of a major Center for Modern and Contemporary Art.

Via di Città ends in **Piazza Postierla** also dubbed "Quattro Cantoni" (the Four Corners), where a marble col-

Residence of the Medici Governor;
above: *Palazzo Piccolomini, "delle Papesse".*

umn, topped by a modern marble statue of the *she-wolf* by Giuliano Vangi marks the Terziere di Città. The modern *little bronze fountain* with an eagle at the top (sculptor Bruno Buracchini), in the square, is one of the seventeen fountains at which the contrade's babies are given their «Contrada Baptism». The little fountain of the Quattro Cantoni is, in fact, where the children of the Noble Contrada of the Eagle are "baptized" and become full-fledged citizens of the contrada. One of the four corners of the square, the one on the left, towards Via del

Palazzo Chigi-Piccolomini alla Postierla and Palazzo del Capitano.

Capitano, is formed by the two façades of **Palazzo Chigi** then **Piccolomini** (or *Palazzo Chigi-Piccolomini alla Postierla*), which is where the *Superintendent for the Artistic and Historical Assets of Siena and Grosseto* is quartered. The splendid mansion was commissioned by Scipione Chigi, towards the second half of the XVI century probably to designs by the painter, sculptor and architect Bartolommeo Neroni, known as "il Riccio". There are two more imposing buildings on Via del Capitano: on the right we have the **Residence of the Medici Governor**, which is used as the Prefecture and as headquarters of the *Provincial Administration*; on the left, the stony façade of **Palazzo del Capitano**, first built at the end of the XIII century as the headquarters of the War Captain and of the Captain of Justice. Like many other Medieval Sienese mansions, this one also underwent major restorations. In 1854, the architect Giulio Rossi headed the restoration project, with totally gratuitous modifications and embellishments to the façade. The ground floor is divided by nine Sienese ogival arches. The upper floor has nine double-mullioned windows. The armorial devices and battlements have all been remade or even invented.

Via del Capitano leads into Piazza del Duomo, that is dominated by the marble bulk of one of the most splendid and famous examples of Italian Romanesque-Gothic cathedral architecture. The church we see today (or rather the slightly smaller version formerly constructed on this site) replaced the IX century **Cathedral of Santa Maria**, built according to a reliable tradition, on the site of a temple dedicated to Minerva.

The façade of the new building that is also dedicated to Our Lady

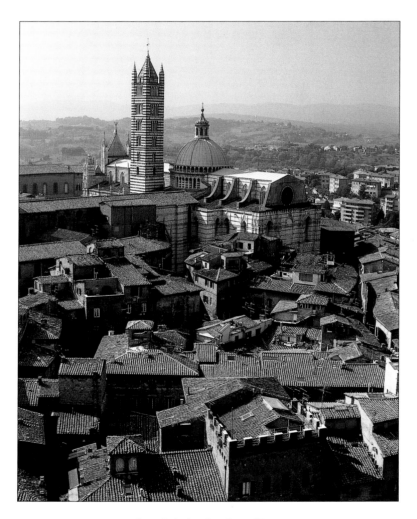

The cathedral and rooftops of Siena.

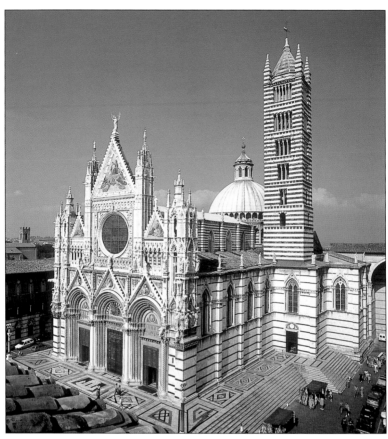

The cathedral;
opposite: *the façade.*

of the Assumption, and is much larger than the IX century structure, faced towards the Ospedale di Santa Maria della Scala (as it is today). Tradition, supported by fairly credible documentation, affirms that the holy edifice was consecrated with due solemnity on 18 November 1179. This building, too, however, except for the crypt, was totally restructured and enlarged from around 1215-20. The work was done little by little, in order not to interrupt regular services

1. Bell tower
2. Main altar
3. Chapel of the Vow
4. Sacristy
5. Pulpit by Nicola and Giovanni Pisano
6. Chapel of St. John the Baptist
7. The Piccolomini Library
8. Piccolomini Altar

and worship. Moreover, from 1316 onwards, the transept and apse were extended even further. The **bell tower** had already been grafted onto an existing, short, tower-house belonging to the Bisdomini-Forteguerri family. The **dome** was finished in 1263, when it was covered with lead sheeting and Rosso Padellaio's "apple" or gilded copper sphere was placed on top, (the lantern was added much later 1667 - in the "style" of the cathedral). Today's art critics, basing their opinions on the similarities between the sculptures and decorations of as the capitals in the front of the cathedral, the triple window and corbels inside the drum and the work of Nicola Pisano, maintain that the cathedral itself was designed by the Apulian-Pisan artist. The lower part of the façade was both designed and decorated with statuary by Nicola's son, the great Giovanni Pisano, who started working on the project in 1285. The extension of the transept and

The interior of the cathedral;
left: *the left side, exterior.*

the elongation of the cathedral towards the choir started, it seems, towards 1316 and continued slowly until about 1339. The work encountered so many technical and stylistic obstacles that in 1332 a

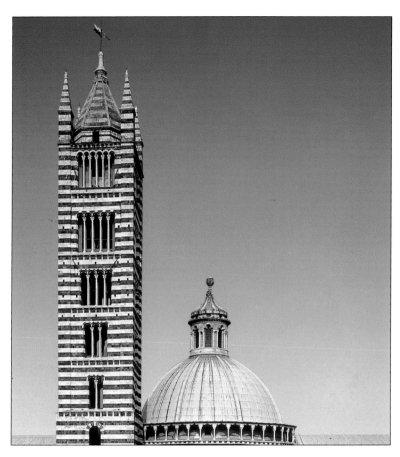

The bell tower;
right: *the dome.*

commission headed by Lorenzo
Maitani, master builder of the
Cathedral of Orvieto, decreed that
it would be better to rebuild a new
church "pulchra magnia et mag-
nifica". The seed for the most ambitious and foolhardy enterprise
ever undertaken by the Sienese
had been sown, but many years
were to elapse before it germinated.
It was only on 23 August 1339, in
fact, that the General Council of
the Bell (Consiglio Generale della

The unfinished façade;
left: *Piazza Jacopo della Quercia.*

Campana) decreed the construction of a vast new temple, in which the existing cathedral was to be included as its transept. The first stone had already been laid some months before and work had started on the three gigantic aisles of the front section which continued up to the Manetti or Santa Maria terrace (piano) and were enclosed by the façade or "Facciatone". The ambitious plans of the Sienese were however disrupted first of all by the terrible Back Death of 1348, which decimated the population and finally by the collapse of certain essential parts of the construction due to irremediable technical deficiencies, so much so, that in June 1357 the governors of the Republic were not only forced to decree the discontinuation of all work on the New Cathedral, but even had to order the destruction of all parts in danger of collapsing.

Important remains of the imposing temple are still visible today in the roofless area to the left of the existing cathedral (known as **Piazza Jacopo della Quercia**), with the columns of the three aisles, its unfinished façade and a part of the left side, where a magnificent doorway (the most beautiful Sienese Gothic doorway and one of the finest in Italy) opens onto the steep staircase leading down to the Baptistry of San Giovanni. After interrupting the construction of the new cathedral, the Sienese turned their attention once more to the old church, which reverted, this time definitely, to its role of Cathedral of Siena. Its façade was only completed towards the end of the XIV century. Work on it recommenced in 1377, under the Master builder Giovanni di Cecco, who attempted to superimpose a late-Gothic top section with the cen-

The Chapel of the Vow.

tral rose window and three cusps upon the lower and order late-Romanesque section, spoiling the harmonious development of Giovanni Pisano's architectural elements with the inert spread of the upper section which certainly owes much of its appearance to the Orvieto cathedral façade. Giovanni Pisano, together with helpers and followers, produced a whole series of marble statues of *Saints, Prophets,*

Sybils and *Allegorical Beasts which weave admirably and harmo*niously in and out of the design of the lower façade. The figures we see today are nearly all copies of the originals, which have been taken down and placed in the ground floor room in the Museo dell'Opera del Duomo. The great spiraled columns, carved by Giovanni Pisano that used to support the main doorway, have been recently removed to the Crypt of the Statues below and will be replaced by copies. The architrave, sculpted by Tino di Camaino, a follower of Giovanni (c. 1297-1300), represents scenes from the *Life of the Infant Mary with St. Joachim and St. Anne.* The bronze doors with the Glorification of the Virgin are an unpretentious recent work by Enrico Manfrini (1958). Three mediocre mosaic panels by Augusto Castellani to designs by Luigi Mussini and Alessandro Franchi (1877) were set into the cusps at the top of the façade during the XIX century. The mosaics, representing the *Coronation of the Virgin*, the *Birth* and the P*resentation of the Virgin at the Temple*, replaced three gilded bronze reliefs that had been made for the three cusps in 1635. At either end of the parvis, stands a column, bearing a She-wolf feeding the Twins, one attributed to the workshop of Giovanni Pisano, the other to Urbano da Cortona (the originals replaced by copies, are also in the Museo dell'Opera). The evocative, severely majestic *interior of the cathedral* is enhanced by the for-

est of black and white marble striped pillars - the colors of Siena's "Balzana" or arms - which is a motif repeated both inside and outside the building. The black and white marble creates an impression of structural solidity, as well as providing a pictorial chiaroscuro effect, that attenuates the vertical surge of the pillars surmounted by their rounded Romanesque-like arches. Before looking at the various works of art in the church, we should, at this point, pause to admire the unique artistic achievement we are actually standing on, and that covers the whole floor of the cathedral, like some fabulous **carpet**: the 52 panels of inlaid, etched and colored marble. The scenes in the central nave, starting from the entrance, depict *Hermes Trismegistus* (designed by Giovanni di Stefano), *the Sienese She-wolf with the Symbols of the cities allied with Siena* (XIV century), the *Wheel* with the *Imperial Eagle* (XIV century), the *Hill of Virtue* (designed by Pintoricchio); the *Wheel of Fortune and Power* (designed by Domenico di Niccolò?). The side aisles contain the figures of the Sybils. Except for the well-conserved Hill of Virtues, very little is left of the original panels. The scenes beneath the dome, in the transept and in the apse are much better preserved. The greatest Sienese artists of the XV and XVI centuries all contributed designs to this remarkable enterprise. Great scenes teeming with hundreds of figures against the bristling towers of fortified towns and idyllic landscapes unfold beneath our feet. The scenes are partly covered with wooden planks to protect them from the daily wear and tear inflicted by the feet of thousands of visitors and worshippers. Among the scenes always left uncovered is the one showing the *Slaughter of the Innocents*, designed by Matteo di Gio-

The apse with the main altar.

The apse, the stained glass window, by Duccio.

vanni (1482) and restored in 1790. It is probably the most admired scene on the whole floor, because of its vivid colors and spectacular representation of violent movement.

We can best admire the impressive and lavish interior from the end of the middle aisle. Beneath the gallery there is an endless and somewhat boring line of *popes' heads*, attributed (together with the equally lengthy series of *emperors'* busts) to the workshop of Giovanni di Stefano: they are terra-cotta busts molded in the workshop and fired in the kilns of the Mazzaburroni family starting in 1495 and decorated at the beginning of the XVI century.

The asymmetrical *dome* is supported by six great piers. The two wooden beams resting on the two *central piers* are supposed to have come from the "Carroccio" (War Standard Chariot) used during the Battle of Montaperti (1260). Six gigantic gilded plaster statues of *St. Catherine, St. Bernardino* and the other four *Patron Saints* of Siena stand on top of the six piers. The right transept starts with the Chapel

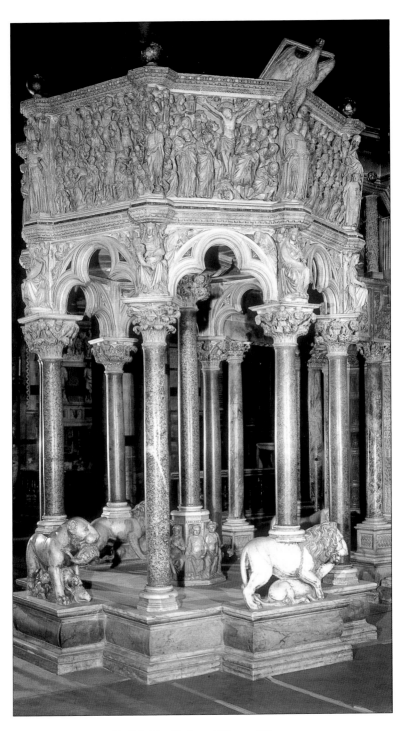

The Pulpit by Nicola and Giovanni Pisano.

43

of the Vow, commissioned by Pope Alexander VII (Chigi) and probably designed by Gian Lorenzo Bernini, who was also one of the supervisors of the construction of the Chapel (1659-63). The plan is circular; the Madonna and Child, venerated by the Sienese as the *Madonna of the Vow* (del Voto), above the altar, is the central portion of a much larger (no longer extant) painting attributed to the workshop of Guido da Siena (c. 1270). The lavishness of the chapel is decidedly Roman Baroque. The *shrine* surrounding the venerated XIII century image, the *gilded bronze angels* and all the *decorations* were designed by Ercole Ferrata of Rome and cast by Giovanni Artusi, called Piscina. The two large marble statues in the niches at the entrance are masterpieces by Bernini, himself, carved in Rome, between 1662 and 1663. They represent the *Magdalen* and *St. Jerome*.

The *Presbiterium* of the cathedral is on a slightly higher level than the aisles and is dominated by the centrally placed imposing marble and bronze **High Altar**, upon which stands Vecchietta's magnificent bronze ciborium (1472). Two bronze *candle-bearing angels* stand near the top of the steps leading up to the altar. They are the last admirable works cast by Sassetta's son Giovanni di Stefano (1489). Francesco di Giorgio and Giacomo Cozzarelli made the other two *bronze angels* at the bottom of the steps in 1490 endowing them with the same airy weightlessness that

they gave the two *little bronze cherub-busts* (called "little spirits") that project from the great masks each side of the altar. Eight other bronze angels cast in 1551 by D. Beccafumi, stand at the side pillars.

The stained glass rose-window above the apse is of great interest, because of its artistic merits and because it is one of the earliest known examples of Italian stained glass. Carli dates it around 1288 and attributes the cartoon to Duccio, as do many other critics, although some scholars see evidence of the hands of Cimabue and a helper. It used to be in the old apse and was transferred to the new one in 1865. It is divided into nine sections depicting the *Burial*, the *Assumption*, the *Coronation of the Virgin, the Four Evangelists, the Four Patron Saints Ansanus, Savinius, Crescentius* and *Bartholomew*. It is almost a miracle that, after so many centuries of wars and destruction, such an extremely fragile masterpiece should have survived to shed its rainbow light on one of the most beautiful cathedrals in the world. The **choir** (except for the XVI century choir-stalls in the apse semicircle) replaces a much earlier XIII century choir, that has been lost. Francesco del Tonghio started working on it alone in 1362 and his son Giacomo joined him in his labors in 1378. Due to XVI century restructuring of the apse, a lot of the earlier ornamentation was unfortunately lost. The last important work on the choir, was done in 1813, when the inlaid mar-

A columniferous lion supports the pulpit by Giovanni Pisano.

quetry panels by Fra Giovanni da Verona were removed from the magnificent early XVI century choir stalls (which are still preserved in the Abbey church of Monte Oliveto Maggiore near Siena) and attached to the XIV century stalls in the Siena cathedral. An interesting and little known piece of Baroque sculpture can be seen in the *vestibule*, next to the sacristy: the *bronze bust of Alexander VII Chigi*, by Piscina. Beyond the **sacristy**, decorated with frescoes attributed to Benedetto di Bindo (1212), we enter the **Chapter Hall**, hung *with portraits of Sienese popes and bishops*.

Back in the left transept of the cathedral, we find the staggeringly beautiful **pulpit** by Nicola and Giovanni Pisano, the most superb masterpiece in the Cathedral of Siena. A veritable milestone in the history of Italian art, it was, to paraphrase Adolfo Venturi, «the Word of the new art made visible». The great marble complex, covered with figures illustrating the history of the Redemption of Mankind, was started in Pisa by Nicola on 29 September 1265 and continued in Siena the following year. It was completed by 6 November 1268. Nicola Pisano was helped by his son Giovanni, Arnolfo di Cambio, Donato and Lapo. The three greatest sculptors of their time, Nicola, Giovanni and Arnolfo, worked side by side on this incomparable masterpiece, which although inspired by Nicola's own hexagonal pulpit in the Pisa Baptistery, is so much richer and more complex (about 307 human figures or heads plus about 70 animal figures or heads have been counted) as well as being less classical and more fervently human in the intense expressive qualities of the faces and attitudes of the figures. A vibrant chiaroscuro and a decided plasticity enhance the profound drama of the scenes (specially where Giovanni's chisel dug into the gleaming marble). The seven main panels on the balustrade, divided by the figures of the *Vir-*gin, *Christ, St. Paul*, the *Evangelists* and *Trumpet-blowing Angels* are representations of Episodes in the Life of the Redeemer: the *Nativity*, the *Adoration of the Magi, Presentation at the Temple, the Flight into Egypt, Slaughter of the Innocents, Crucifixion*, the *Elect*, and the *Damned.*

In the left transept, opposite the Chapel of the Vow, we find the **Chapel of St. John the Baptist**, commissioned by the Rector of the Cathedral Works, Alberto Aringhieri, in 1492, as a worthy *receptacle for the relic* of the Baptist's Arm, preserved in a splendid XV century silver reliquary and donated to Siena by Pope Pius II. The chapel was probably designed by Giovanni di Stefano and has a circular floor plan.

The magnificent marble *doorway* with statues and reliefs was carved by Marrina but the bases of the two *columns*, richly decorated with classical motifs,

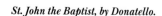
St. John the Baptist, by Donatello.

The Piccolomini Library with frescoes by Pintoricchio.

are by Antonio Federighi and Giovanni di Stefano. The elegant bronze *gate* is by Sallustio Barili. The great statue of St. *John the Baptist* by Donatello dominates the Chapel from its niche opposite the entrance. It resembles the wooden St. John in Santa Maria Gloriosa dei Frari in Venice and the wooden Magdalen of the Florentine Baptistry. The same dramatic feeling emerges from all their haggard faces, emaciated flesh and from the ragged locks of their hair and hairshirts. In the middle of the chapel there is an octagonal *mar-*

ble holy water stoup with eight bas-relief panels by Antonio Federighi (1460). The episodes depicted are: *Creation of Adam and Eve, Temptation of Eve, Appearance of the Almighty, the Expulsion from Eden, Hercules and the Lion, Cacus fighting a Centaur. Cherubs, dolphins, dragons* etc., decorate the base.

We now come to another magnificent architectural, sculptural and frescoed complex made for the cathedral, known as the **Piccolomini Library**. It was commissioned in 1492 by the Archbishop of Siena, Francesco Cardinal Piccolomini Todeschini (later Pope Pius III), who wished to create a worthy receptacle for the fabulous book collection put together by his uncle Pius II, who had died in 1464. The arch on the left, and the bronze *door* by Antoniolo di Giacomo led into the Library, which was never actually used for Pius II's books, but which was dazzlingly frescoed by Pintoricchio all over its ceiling (1502-03) and walls (1505-1507) after the death of pope Pius III. With the help of a large group of helpers, Pintoricchio recounted the more salient events in the Life of Pius II. The picturesque and colorfully portrayed events seize both the humble pilgrim and the scholar with delight. Hundreds of figures mostly in rainbow-hued ceremonial robes (the tints of which are so perfectly preserved, that they seem to have just been painted), throng the walls and are somewhat emotionless but nonetheless spectacular.

The ceiling is decorated in the Roman Renaissance fashion with "grotesques" arranged around the Piccolomini coat of arms. The ten scenes on the walls, starting from the end, right of the window, are:

The Ascension of Christ, by Girolamo da Cremona.

The Piccolomini Altar with four statues by Michelangelo.

Enea Silvio Piccolomini, aged 27, leaving for Basle; oration in front of James I of Scotland; Frederick III crowns him Poet Laureate; he bows in submission before the true pope Eugenius IV; as Bishop of Siena he meets Frederick III, betrothed to Eleonora of Portugal at the Camollia Gate of Siena;he is made Cardinal by pope Callixtus III; he is crowned Pope Pius II and his official entrance into the Lateran Basilica; Pius II assembles the Christian princes in Mantua, for the Crusade against the Turks, Pius II canonizes the deceased St. Catherine of Siena, on 29 June 1461 (it is said that the youth on the left, in the foreground is a portrait of Raphael and the likeness is in effect quite noticeable); *Arrival of Pius II, already very ill, at the harbor of Ancona to meet the Venetian fleet before its departure for the Crusade.* He was to die in Ancona, on 15 August 1464 after waiting in vain for the fleet to arrive.

Vasari states that the cartoons for the frescoes were prepared by Raphael. Three drawings in the Uffizi seem to confirm this theory. The marble group of the **Three Graces** in the center of the Library has been recently restored. It was brought from Rome by Cardinal Todeschini and donated to the Library. It is considered one of the best Roman copies (among the eight known to be in existence) of a Greek painted or sculpted original. The most admired objects in the room, after Pintoricchio's frescoes, are the great missals and antiphonaries, in the glass cases beneath the frescoes. The dazzlingly illuminated pages, done partly by great masters of the art such as Liberale di Verona and Girolamo da Cremona can be considered some of the finest examples of the great Italian illuminators' art of the XV century.

As we continue our tour of the cathedral we see four statues by Michelangelo Buonarroti on the great marble frontal, known as the **Piccolomini Altar**. Cardinal Piccolomini Todeschini, himself, commissioned it from the Lombard artist Andrea Bregno (c. 1480), who worked on it with some of his pupils until his death (1501), embellishing it with carved statues and reliefs that recall the works in Santa Maria del Popolo in Rome. It was probably the death of Bregno that induced Cardinal Todeschini to order 15 statues first from Pietro Torrigiani and then from Michelangelo, who, between 1503 and 1504, carved the statues of *St. Peter, St. Paul, St. Pius* and *St. Gregory* The statues are some of Michelangelo's less known works and we must admit that notwithstanding the plentiful and detailed documentation identifying them as his production, they show Michelangelo at his weakest and most uncertain, which may be due to the fact that he used helpers (specially in the case of St. Pius and St. Gregory). Both St. Peter and St. Paul are more typical of Michelangelo's style, in their vibrant torsion and in the expressive power that seem to herald the dominant force of the Moses of San Pietro in Vincoli in Rome.

OSPEDALE DI S. MARIA DELLA SCALA

The long, low façade of the **Archbishop's Palace** runs along the left side of Piazza del Duomo (if one is looking at the cathedral façade). Before 1660 it was the residence of the Rector of the Cathedral Works as well as of the Cathedral Canons, and was connected to the cathedral by a loggia. Opposite the Cathedral is the lengthy façade of the Ospedale di Santa Maria della Scala. This august charitable institution was founded by the cathedral canons in the IX century, although the first parchment document in which it is officially mentioned dates from 1090. At first, it was merely a hospice, but by the X century it was already a hospital run by the Canons and later by lay brothers (Oblates) directed by Comptroller or Rector. The name of Santa Maria della Scala certainly derives from the fact that it abuts on the stairs ("scale" in Italian) leading up

A double-lighted window on the façade of the Ospedale;
above, from the left: *the Archbishop's Palace; Ospedale de S. Maria della Scala.*

The old sacristy with frescoes by Vecchietta;
below: ***Building the Hospital** by Domenico di Bartolo in the "pilgrims' hall".*

The "pilgrims' hall";
below: *The Marriage of the Foundlings, by Domenico di Bartolo.*

Granting the Statutes, by Domenico di Bartolo, in the "pilgrims' hall".

to the parvis of Santa Maria, the cathedral. The building is immense, practically a city within the city, where for nearly a thousand years each century has brought additions and changes, although the richly frescoed old XIV-XV century nucleus has been preserved. Two, highly interesting rooms have been converted into a museum: the **old sacristy**, that is entirely decorated with frescoes by Vecchietta and the large **"pilgrims' hall"**. The frescoes in this room, by Vecchietta, Priamo della Quercia and Domenico di Bartolo around 1444, portray the *glory*, the *power* and the *charitable deeds* of the hospital. This fresco cycle one of the few dealing with a secular-civic theme is,

The Church of the Hospital:
Resurrected Christ (1476) by Vecchietta.

therefore, of exceptional artistic and historical interest. The present **Church of the Hospital**, dedicated to Our Lady of the Assumption, is an enlarged, or rather totally reconstructed XV century edition of a much smaller Medieval church. The airy, simple interior fits beautifully into the aisleless Sienese Renaissance structure, reminiscent of the Franciscan Gothic tradition. The high altar, a fascinating architectural and sculptural complex, bears an imposing bronze *Resurrected Christ* (1476) by Vecchietta, that replaces the ciborium by the same artist, that was transferred to the high altar of the cathedral in 1506. The statue is one of the finest of the Sienese Renaissance. It has a dramatic strength reminiscent of Donatello, combined with exquisite anatomical technique and vigorous luminous qualities. The two bronze *angel candelabra* on the steps below were cast (1585) by Accursio Baldi da Monte San Savino, earning Giambologna's admiration and praise. The spacious *apse semicircle*, once frescoed by Francesco di Giorgio Martini was enlarged and refrescoed in 1732 by the Neapolitan painter Sebastiano Conca, who painted the *Pool of Bethesda* in a perspective colonnade. A little door leads out of the choir into the sacristy-treasure vault, where a large number of relics are kept in precious gold or silver *reliquaries* made by Byzantine (XI-XII century) and XV-XVI century Sienese goldsmiths.

MUSEO ARCHEOLOGICO NAZIONALE DI SIENA

Some of the rooms of the Ospedale di S. Maria della Scala house the **Museo Archeologico Nazionale di Siena** (the entrance is from Piazza del Duomo and the corner of Via del Capitano). The museum contains hundreds of objects of outstanding artistic-historical interest from the prehistoric, Etruscan and Roman periods that were collected throughout the area surrounding Siena.

Etruscan fibula; above: *Etruscan pottery, IV century BC.*

MUSEO DELL'OPERA DEL DUOMO

The right aisle of the New Cathedral was transformed, as early as the XV century into the headquarters of the Opera (Cathedral Works). Nearly all the rooms inside are now used for the Museo dell'Opera del Duomo, which is chiefly famous for Giovanni Pisano's marble statues and for the great altarpiece with Duccio di Buoninsegna's Maestà Altarpiece. Most of the

ground floor is occupied by architectural fragments and by the great marble statues carved by Giovanni (1284-96) and his followers for the cathedral façade: strong dramatic figures of *Prophets, Sybils, Philosophers*, impetuously launched forward or drawn back, with powerful muscles draped in flowing robes. An awesome concert of violently agitated figures, that nearly all express tragedy or terror, in gesture or expression *Moses, Plato, Simeon, Elijah, Balaam, Miriam, Habbakkuk*. Even the animals seem to explode with tension in the complexity of their violent, almost tragic masks that belong to a lost world of giants. The **Duccio Room**, upstairs, can almost be termed a Holy of Holies of Sienese painting. After

St. Simeon, by Giovanni Pisano (detail).

Maestà by Duccio di Buoninsegna (front).

many vicissitudes, the imposing Duccio **Maestà** has been placed here. It was commissioned from Duccio on the 9 October 1308 and the great panel was painted on both sides with a predella and cusp de-

The Kiss of Judas, detail of Maestà (back).

stipulated. The front panel shows the *Virgin Mary*, Protectress of Siena, *with her Son on her knees, seated on a throne and surrounded by a throng of Angels and Saints*. The first four kneeling figures are the Patron Saints of Siena: *Saints Ansanus, Savinius, Crescentius and Victor*. The predella contains seven little scenes from the *Life of the Virgin and the Infancy of Christ spaced by the figures of Prophets*. The cusps are decorated with further *Episodes from the Life of the Virgin*. The other side, that used to face the choir, contains many *Scenes from the Life of Christ*. Even in its present stripped state, Duccio's Maestà is still one of the turning points of European culture at the beginning of the XIV century, when profound transformations affected every aspect of Western cultural mores. Where Giotto or Dante and even Giovanni Pisano opened-up vistas of unhoped-for human, albeit dra-

corations on both sides as well. Nearly all the painting was done by Duccio himself, as the contract

Noli me tangere, detail of the Maestà (back).

Central detail of the Maestà.

The Nativity of the Virgin, by Pietro Lorenzetti.

matic, earthly understanding, Duccio turned his attention towards a musical harmony between heaven and earth, shaking off the chains that had hitherto bound painting and Byzantine culture in general and directed his art towards more concrete form, both in his transcendent poetic dreams of divine light, which he expresses in the gleaming gold and lucid purity of his colors, as well as in the human reality of his solidly composed figures and their severely solemn expressions. Another masterpiece from the cathedral is preserved in the Duccio Room: the *Birth of the Virgin*, by Pietro Lorenzetti, signed and dated 1342. Pietro almost anticipates the perspective studies of the following century and offers us a scene that is based on wisely measured space (breaking with the triptych tradition) and each figure is portrayed in a combination of grace and solemnity. St. Anne is

Virgin and Child, a very early painting by Duccio di Buoninsegna.

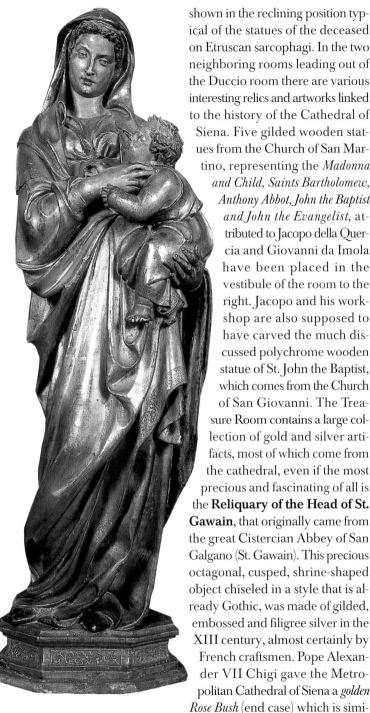

shown in the reclining position typical of the statues of the deceased on Etruscan sarcophagi. In the two neighboring rooms leading out of the Duccio room there are various interesting relics and artworks linked to the history of the Cathedral of Siena. Five gilded wooden statues from the Church of San Martino, representing the *Madonna and Child, Saints Bartholomew, Anthony Abbot, John the Baptist and John the Evangelist*, attributed to Jacopo della Quercia and Giovanni da Imola have been placed in the vestibule of the room to the right. Jacopo and his workshop are also supposed to have carved the much discussed polychrome wooden statue of St. John the Baptist, which comes from the Church of San Giovanni. The Treasure Room contains a large collection of gold and silver artifacts, most of which come from the cathedral, even if the most precious and fascinating of all is the **Reliquary of the Head of St. Gawain**, that originally came from the great Cistercian Abbey of San Galgano (St. Gawain). This precious octagonal, cusped, shrine-shaped object chiseled in a style that is already Gothic, was made of gilded, embossed and filigree silver in the XIII century, almost certainly by French craftsmen. Pope Alexander VII Chigi gave the Metropolitan Cathedral of Siena a *golden Rose Bush* (end case) which is similar to, the one given by Pope Pius

Wooden Virgin, by Jacopo della Quercia.

II Piccolomini to the Senate of the Sienese Republic in 1458, although it is more elaborate in the branches, leaves and roses.

The last two rooms of the museum have been placed almost at the end of the left aisle of the "New Cathedral" so that we have a close-up view of the windows and magnifi- cent capitals on the black and white pillars that were incorporated into the walls. The last room of the Museo dell'Opera contains a number of paintings, some of which can be considered absolute masterpieces. It is called the room of the *Madonna of the large eyes (occhi grossi)* or Madonna of the Victory of Montaperti. The importance to Siena of this venerable relic (the central part of an altarpiece) is certainly significant, if, as appears likely, this was the image on the high altar of the cathedral, in front of which the Sienese vowed they would present the keys of the city to the Virgin (on the eve of the Battle of Montaperti, 4 September 1260) if they should be victorious against the Florentines, which in fact they were. Two other fine paintings in this room are the delightful little panels by

Reliquary of St. Gawain and detail.

Madonna of the Large Eyes by the Maestro di Tressa.

Sano di Pietro (c. 1444), *showing St. Bernardino preaching in Piazza San Francesco and in Piazza del Campo.* The latter is particularly fascinating, because the scene in front of Palazzo Pubblico is as minutely detailed, as an illuminated manuscript, with its groups of nobles and commoners, listening devoutly to the saint. The larger group of the women is separated from the men by a long red curtain; the white shawls and veils draped over their heads half conceal splendid long, embroidered red, black or green gowns. Sano even painted the shutters on the

*The crown of St. Gawain, by a Sienese artist (early XIV century)
and the staff of St. Gawain, Sienese goldsmith (1320, circa).*

windows, which enabled
people to see, without being seen, as well as the famous enclosure with its
ladder, where a live she-
wolf was kept as a symbol
of the mythical origins
of Siena.

St. Bernardino Preaching, by Sano di Pietro.

After the apse of the Cathedral was lengthened, abutting on the cliff over Valle Piatta, great arches were built beneath it, starting in 1316, underneath which, like a crypt, the church of San Giovanni Battista was created. This new structure that was used as the Baptistry of Siena was probably designed by Camaino di Crescentino. The six vaults of the cathedral above were completed after the work on the new cathedral was suspended, whilst the decoration of the façade of San Giovanni was continued for decades, under the direction of Domenico di Agostino, starting in 1355. The top part of the façade was never finished, but the rest is in pure Sienese Gothic style, with three deeply splayed jambed doorways, above which runs a gallery of arches and a frieze supporting three great twin ogival mullioned windows (1355).The three graffito scenes on the floor of the parvis portray

The cathedral apse and façade of the baptistry.

the *Birth of a Child*, the *Baptism* and the *Blessing* (or Confirmation?) of *Six Children.*

The interior of San Giovanni is rectangular, divided into three aisles by two large pillars. All the vaults were completely frescoed in the XV century; the most remarkable frescoes are the ones covering the central vault, by Vecchietta (1450), depicting the *Apostles* and the *Articles of the Creed.* The great masterpiece, that makes Siena the envy of the world, however, is the **Baptismal Font** in the center of the church. It has often been called the "oldest anthology of early Italian Renaissance sculpture." In addition to contributions by a number of less famous artists, this masterpiece is the work of the hands of three of the greatest sculptors of the time Donatello, Lorenzo Ghiberti and Jacopo della Quercia. The base consists of two great hexagonal marble steps; the marble font itself is hexagonal too, the six sides, separated from each other by six gilded bronze figures of the *Virtues* contain six gilded bronze panels depicting Episodes from the Life of St. John the Baptist in chronological order: *Zacharias being told of the forthcoming birth of the Baptist* (Jacopo della Quercia); statuette of *Justice* (Giovanni di Turino); *Birth of the Baptist* (Turino di Sano and Giovanni di Turino); statuette of *Charity* (Giovanni di Turino); the *Baptist Preaching* (Giovanni di Turino), statuette of *Prudence* (Giovanni di Turino), the

Baptismal font; below: *detail of the panel with Jacopo della Quercia's Annunciation to Zacharias.*

Baptismal font, detail of the panel portraying the Baptist before Herod by Lorenzo Ghiberti.

Baptism of Christ (Lorenzo Ghiberti); *Faith* (Donatello); the *Baptist before Herod* (Lorenzo Ghiberti); *Hope* (Donatello); the *Head of the Baptist presented to Herod* (Donatello); and *Fortitude* (Goro di Neroccio). The most impressive of all the scenes is the Donatello relief: a vortex with the head of the Baptist in the center, draws the figures together yet freezes their movements. It creates a dramatic feeling that is echoed, after the perspective hiatus of the laden tables, by the tragic stupor of the observers on the right. In the background, in an incredible perspective fugue created with a depth of but a few millimeters, the life of the court continues unperturbed, acted out by timeless figures, under the receding arches.

PINACOTECA NAZIONALE

As we walk back along Via del Capitano, we will come to Piazza Postierla and the beginning of Via di San Pietro. The two mansions which used to belong to the Brigidi and Buonsignori families have now become the Pinacoteca Nazionale (National Picture Gallery),

The Madonna of the Franciscans, by Duccio; opposite: *Palazzo Buonsignori, home of the Pinacoteca Nazionale.*

Beato Agostino Novello, by Simone Martini.

one of the greatest Italian Museums, especially for the "fondi oro" or paintings on golden backgrounds of the Sienese XIV and XV centuries. The Sienese painting tradition from Duccio di Buoninsegna to the Lorenzetti, from Simone Mar-

From the top: *Annunciation by Ambrogio Lorenzetti; the Last Judgment (detail) by Giovanni di Paolo; View of a City, attributed to Sassetta (formerly attributed to A. Lorenzetti).*

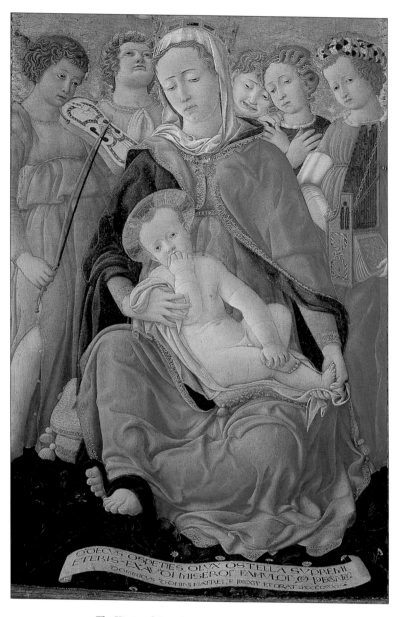

The Virgin of Humility, by Domenico di Bartolo.

tini to Sassetta, Francesco di Giorgio or Giovanni di Paolo (including Neroccio, Matteo di Giovanni, Sodoma and Beccafumi) is presented in chronological order, offering a fabulous series of masterpieces and minor works and a unique insight into the evolution of painting in Siena. The events that led up to the formation of this important collection came to a head on 15 May, 1930 when a decree was issued officially

Virgin and Child by Neroccio;
left: *Annunciation by Francesco di Giorgio Marini.*

authorizing the transfer of the National Picture Gallery of Siena to its present site in Via San Pietro. The Buonsignori palace, however, already appears too small for the size and importance of the collection. The authorities are considering transferring the works to the Ospedale di Santa Maria della Scala, in Piazza del Duomo, which is already a museum in itself. A tour of the Pinacoteca Nazionale of Siena starts on the second floor. Further information on the works in the gallery can be obtained from: P. Torriti, *La Pinacoteca Nazionale di Siena, I dipinti dal XII al XV secolo*, Sagep, Genoa 1977, P. Torriti, *La Pinacoteca Nazionale di Siena*, edizione Sagep, Genoa 1990.

Nativity of the Virgin, by Beccafumi.

S. Niccolò al Carmine

Via San Pietro leads into Piazza di Postierla («I quattro Cantoni» or the «Four Corners»). On the corner, opposite Palazzo Borghesi, which used to contain frescoes by Beccafumi (now lost), is a *pharmacy* containing interesting neoclassical furniture, designed by Agostino Fantastici, around 1830. Turning immediately left, we enter *Via di Stalloreggi* ("Stabulae Regis" or "Stables of the king"?), almost completely lined with *Medieval mansions* built of brick or stone (where the towers of the Cacciaconti used to stand), which are often very interesting, as they

Arch of the two doors; below: *the church of the Carmine.*

have not undergone much restructuring and still preserve most of their original appearance. Midway down the street (at the corner of Via Castelvecchio) there is a shrine with the *Virgin holding the Dead Jesus* (this work by Sodoma is also known as the Virgin of the Crow). At the end of Via Stalloreggi, there is a gateway or arch, in the right pier of which a XVI century *shrine*, surrounded by a delicate stucco frame, encloses a frescoed *Madonna and Child, with Sts. John the Baptist and Catherine of Siena*, attributed to Bartolomeo di David (XVI century). Left of the arch, a plaque indicates that Duccio di Buoninsegna used to live in the house (probably after and not before painting the famous «Maestà», which "was painted in the Muciatti house outside the Stalloreggi gate", according to contemporary sources. The gateway was part of the oldest circle of the town walls and consisted of two great arches (one of which was walled up centuries ago), but the gate is still known as the *Arch of the Two Doors* (Arco delle due Porte). The oldest shrine in the city is set into the outer face of the town wall; it encloses a XIV century frescoed *Madonna and Child*. Leaving the archway, we turn left into the *Pian dei Mantellini* surrounded by churches and fine mansions. Of special note: the great complex of the *Carmelite Monastery* with the adjacent Church of **San Niccolò al Carmine**. The first documented proof of the **Carmelite Order's** presence in Siena and of the foundation of a church of theirs is dated 1262. The existing church was constructed through the XIV, XV and XVI centuries and subjected to restoration and additions up to the present. The restored **Cloister** (Nr. 44), built at the end of the XVI century, contains frescoes by Giuseppe Nicola Nasini (1710) depicting scenes illustrating the *Carmelite Rule*. The **bell tower** recently attributed to Peruzzi, actually seems to date from XVI century, although some scholars consider it a XVII century structure. The Carmelite Church, has remained reasonably intact in spite of the XIX century expropriations, and the radical restructuring at the beginning of the XX century and contains many works of art. See especially: the large panel by Domenico Beccafumi, showing *St. Michael pursuing the rebellious angels*, painted before 1535 and a second, expurgated version of the unfinished panel, now in the Pinacoteca Nazionale, both of which are, at any rate, fundamentally important works of the Tuscan Mannerist school. The predella underneath is not original, but a mediocre contribution by Stefano

Church of the Carmine; The Expulsion of the Rebellious Angels, by Beccafumi.

Volpi. The sacristy contains a beautiful polychrome terracotta statue of *St. Sigismund*, attributed rightly to Giacomo Cozzarelli in his later years (c. 1506).

The Carmelite Church stands near the turning from Pian dei Mantellini into *Via della Diana*, which takes its name from the spring that was sought for in vain by the Sienese, as Dante Alighieri recalls. The *Via di S. Marco* is almost parallel to it; at the beginning of the street on the left, is the little Romanesque façade in black and white stone, of the deconsecrated *church of San Marco*, which is now used as a shop.

The intersection of Via di San Marco and Via della Diana is marked by the delightful little XVIII century façade of the **Chapel of Our Lady of the Rosary**. The façade of the chapel is intact and is an interesting example of Sienese Baroque. Romagnoli has attributed its design to Pietro Augusto Montini (1722-23), while Chierici maintains that it was the work of Jacopo Franchini. The travertine Renaissance *well* in front of the chapel was commissioned by Francesco Cardinal Petrucci in 1522.

Via delle Cerchia connects Pian dei Mantellini with the **Prato di Sant'Agostino**, near the *Porta all'Arco* (Gateway of the Arch). It is a typical street that follows the line of the Medieval walls. The imposing bulk of the Church of Sant'Agostino, the apse of which is still Romanesque, was started towards the middle of the XIII century (1258). Construction, however, was still in progress in 1309. We do not know exactly when work was concluded, but we do know that the church was enlarged and restructured between 1450 and 1458/90. Several important traces of this second period are visible on the outer walls of the Augustinian Monastery adjacent to the church, as well as inside the church itself, in the last chapel on the right in the transept, which was restored to its original state a few years ago. The overall impression conveyed by the interior as we see it today, however, is predominantly neoclassical, because of

the work done by Luigi Vanvitelli in 1755, after the disastrous 1747 fire. He renovated the building and endowed it with a sober clarity and austerity of line and decorations that do not to clash with the monumental marble and colored "scagliola" XVI-XVII century altars. One generally enters the church through the little door leading into the left aisle of the church from the "Prato" di Sant'Agostino: it is an excellent vantage point for viewing all

Crucifixion, by Pietro Perugino.

the numerous altar-panels painted by great Italian and (more specifically) Sienese XIII-XVII century masters. The outstanding works include, the *Crucifixion*, by Perugino; the *Baptism of Constantine*, by F. Vanni; the *Holy Trinity*, by P. Sorri; the **Bichi Chapel** frescoed by F. di Giorgio Martini and Signorelli; t**he Piccolomini Chapel** with A. Lorenzetti's *Madonna Enthroned* and the *Adoration of the Magi*, by Sodoma, etc.

Adoration of the Magi, by Sodoma.

Tiled floor (XV cent.) in the Bichi Chapel.

St. Catherine's Birthplace in Fontebranda

Back in Via di Città, we turn into the picturesque *Via della Galluzza*, to get to Fontebranda in the territory of the Noble Contrada dell'Oca (Goose). Fontebranda takes its name from the most famous spring in Siena, but is still more renowned throughout the Catholic world, because it is the birthplace of Saint Catherine of Siena. Her exalted religious fervor even roused Pope Gregory XI from his torpor. She was born in 1347, probably on 25 March to the dyer Jacopo di Benincasa and to Monna Lapa Piagenti. Catherine's name is especially linked to the history of the papacy, which, at that time, was exiled in Avignon. It was the mystical Sienese Saint who did everything in her power to achieve the return of the popes to Rome (1377). Her famous "Epistles", full of ardent mystical passion, that she addressed, as a Sister in Christ, to popes, princes and rulers throughout Europe brought her literary as well as religious fame. She died in Rome on 29 April 1380 and was canonized by the Sienese pope, Pius II Piccolomini in 1461. She

Entrance to the House of St. Catherine.

was proclaimed Joint Patron Saint of Rome in 1866 by Pius XII and Joint Patron Saint of Italy in 1939. She was finally proclaimed Doctor of the Church in 1970 by Pope Paul VI. Catherine's probable birthplace was bought for the City of Siena on the 28 January 1466. The inhabitants of Fontebranda demanded that it be permanently available for public veneration. Later on, the Confraternity of St. Catherine totally transformed the house into a veritable sanctuary, full of memorabilia and works of art dedicated to the memory of the Saint. The original entrance to the Sanctuary of St. Catherine has always been on the *Vicolo del Tiratoio*. The beautiful Renaissance stone doorway is still visible, and the words "SPONSAE KHRISTI CATERINAE DOMUS" are carved into the lintel. Since the ancient parish church of Sant'Antonio was deliberately demolished in order to build the *Portico dei Comuni d'Italia* (1941), the entrance to St. Catherine's House and its oratories has been through the Portico itself, and every year on the first Sunday of May, consecrated oil is offered by a different Italian municipality. The only old part of the complex is the fine travertine XV-

XVI century *well*. Beyond the portico, there is a little loggiaed hallway with slim, elegant columns, generally attributed to Peruzzi. Beyond this hallway, a second *atrium with arches* at the end, links the Oratory of the Crucifix with the **Oratory of the Kitchen**, that was partly built in what was probably the Benincasa kitchen. To start with, the room was the "Catharinate" Confraternity's prayer room; later, in 1546, it was enlarged by encompassing various smaller rooms, whereupon the resulting enlarged chamber was richly frescoed. The **Church** or **Oratory of the Crucifix** houses the XII century Pisan

*The Portico
of the Italian Municipalities, and detail.*

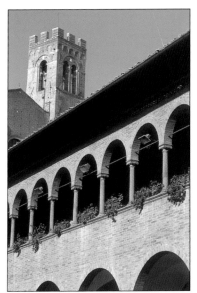

school *Crucifix* that, according to tradition, gave St. Catherine her stigmata. Before leaving this mystical place, we need to mention the old **Fountain of Fontebranda**, which is downhill from the Oratory and next to the gateway named after it. It is the most famous, and the oldest fountain in Siena and its abundantly flowing waters have quenched the thirst of generations of Sienese, ground the flour of countless mills driven by its flow, and provided a livelihood for tanners

A DEMONE LIBERAT

VEXATAM, CATHERINA

The house of St. Catherine: Miracle of the Possessed Women (detail) by Pietro Sorri.

and wool-dyers who belonged to the Wool Guild. It was covered with a vaulted roof in 1246. Considerable sums were spent at various intervals to keep the fountain clean and freely flowing, but chiefly to convey to it the waters from the springs which were gradually dis-covered in other districts, some of them quite distant from Fontebranda. As in all the most important Medieval fountains, the first basin was used for drawing drinking water; the second, fed by the overflow from the first, was the drinking trough for cattle and horses,

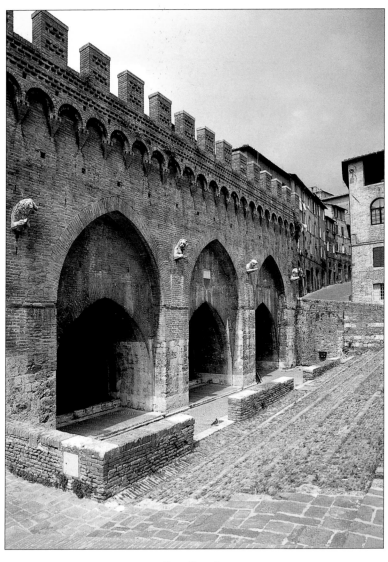

Fonte Branda.

whereas the third was used for laundry. Fontebranda, today, still has its three solid double, slightly pointed arches, enhanced by the red brick walls and by four stone lions.
Via dei Pittori links the St. Catherine complex to *Via delle Terme* from which one can turn into *Via della Sapienza*, and then, go left, onto **Vicolo della Pallacorda**, one of the most typical Medieval alleyways in Siena. The beauty of its somewhat rustic architecture will both surprise and delight the visitor who takes the trouble to make the detour.

BASILICA
OF SAN DOMENICO

Via ella Sapienza ends in the piazza of the Basilica of San Domenico, the construction of which, on the little hill called Camporegio, began around 1225, a few years after the founder of the Order, St. Dominic Guzman had been to Siena (1215?) (his visit is not documented, but is almost certain). The land for the church was donated by Fortebraccio Malavolti and the means were partly supplied by the Municipality of Siena and partly given in alms. The Dominican Church and Monastery must have been completed around 1262-65. The church was enlarged, as the fully Gothic style of the nave and of the transept reveals, towards the middle of the XIV century.

The XIV century structure of the basilica is what we can admire today, even if it was disastrously damaged by a fire in 1443, which reduced it to a skeleton and by another in 1531, which started from a chapel and spread to the whole church. A trussed roof covers the vast aisleless nave, built in accordance with the monastic rule of

*View of
the Basilica of San Domenico.*

the preaching order, so that the faithful and the preacher should not be separated by any structural obstacle. In 1667, the fresco of *St. Catherine and a follower*, unanimously attributed to Andrea Vanni (between 1375 and 1398) was moved to the **Chapel of the Vaults**, which has always been dedicated to the cult of the Sienese saint. Andrea Vanni was a faithful follower of Saint Catherine, who wrote him three letters, so we are moved to believe that the face of the Saint, at least, is the only portrait in existence, painted during her lifetime. Beyond the Chapel of the Vaults, on the right wall of the church, there is a succession of enchanting works of art, such as the *Birth of the Virgin* (1584), one of Alessandro Casolani's most beautiful paintings, justly considered his masterpiece.

The **Chapel of St. Catherine of Siena** was commissioned by Niccolò Bensi in 1460. The head of the Saint, brought here from Rome, in 1384, is the central niche in front

The interior.

of the splendid *marble altar*, sculpted in 1469 by Giovanni di Stefano. It is protected by a gilded grille and flanked by two sculpted candle-bearing angels; above the little window, there is a delicate image of the Saint surrounded by cherubim. The chapel walls are completely covered with frescoes and oil painting murals. The decorative work was begun by Sodoma in 1526 who painted the frescoes of the *Mystical Rapture of St. Catherine and the Ecstasy or Eucharistic Vision of the Saint*. They are two world-famous masterpieces by this ardent painter who managed to effect a poetic

The Chapel of St. Catherine; the Ecstasy of St. Catherine by Sodoma; right: *Tabernacle with the head of the saint, by Giovanni di Stefano.*

blend of perfect draftsmanship with a wise use of color, without ever falling into the trap of illustrative languor. Notwithstanding the restricted space at his disposal, the artist managed to impart a solemn grandeur to the monumental figures. Beyond the chapel, against the wall is the *Adoration of the Shepherds*, by Francesco di Giorgio. This painting is of ex-

Maestà by Guido da Siena.

ceptional interest, not only because of its high quality, but also because it is one of few paintings by this great Sienese architect, sculptor and painter. Painted around 1475-80, it no longer shows the influence of Neroccio, but possesses traits that bring it well within the sphere of Verrocchio, with the incisive lines, classical landscape and energetic realism, which we also see in Francesco di Giorgio's beautiful painting of the Nativity (Pinacoteca Nazionale); all these elements link the Sienese painter to the Florentine Renaissance at the end of the 15th century, between Verrocchio and Botticelli, when Leonardo's sublime spirit was spreading it wings.

The great altarpiece by Benvenuto di Giovanni.

The fifth chapel, where the great *altarpiece* of Guido da Siena used to hang (now in Palazzo Pubblico), at present contains two old Sienese panel paintings; the first shows the *Enthroned Virgin and Child with Angels and Saints Gregory, James, Jerome and Sebastian*, and is one of Benvenuto di Giovanni's best works (1483) with its brilliantly clear gemstone colors that throw the solid, massive figures into relief; the second portrays *St. Barbara enthroned between the Magdalen and St. Catherine of Alexandria*. This recently restored painting is probably Matteo di Giovanni's greatest work (1479); it reveals a supremely luminous quality linked to delicate draftsmanship and a chromatic transparency that the Sienese artist had never before achieved. Matteo also painted the enchanting *Adoration of the Magi* in the lunette above. The left wall of the central nave of the basilica is full of many other works of art, starting from the little painting on the first altar, by Francesco di Vannuccio (c. 1370-80) once attributed to Paolo di Giovanni Fei: it depicts a *Madonna and Child*

and is grafted into the center of a much larger painting, by Sodoma, representing the *Almighty, Saints Vincent, Louis, Catherine of Siena and Sebastian*. Below it, above the altar top, runs a predella divided into various orders, with *15 scenes from the New Testament*, that are somewhat reminiscent of Beccafumi or Riccio, by an unknown XVI century Sienese painter.

Nativity of the Virgin, by Alessandro Casolani.

FORTRESS OF SANTA BARBARA

Leaving San Domenico, and going along Viale dei Mille we reach the site of the former Spanish **fortress** of Don Diego de Mendoza, that was razed to the ground during a popular uprising in 1552, but then rebuilt a little further south by order of Cosimo I de' Medici after the conquest of Siena in 1555. The Grand Duke personally entrusted one of his architects, Baldassarre Lanci from Urbino with the construction, in 1561. This powerful defensive and offensive rectangular structure, is entirely built in brick and supported on an escarped base, surmounted by a thick bulging brick cordon. There are enormous, wedge-shaped bastions on each of the four corners with rounded spurs, surmounted by great *Medici escutcheons.* The extensive and fascinating underground chambers have been transformed into the cellars of the *Enoteca Italica,* which is famous for its Italian wine tasting.

The **public gardens of the Lizza,** opposite the Medici fortress, were laid out in the XIX century.

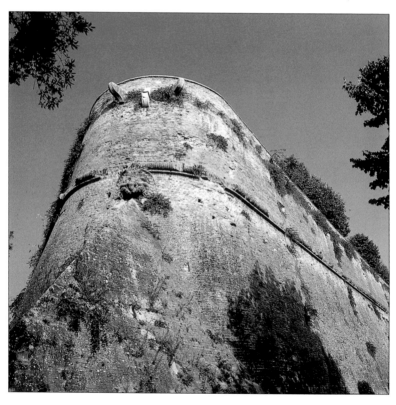

The Medici Fortress, a bastion.

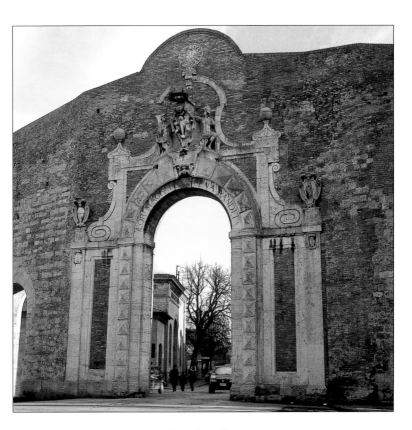

Porta Camollia.

PORTA CAMOLLIA

From the Lizza gardens we take Via Montanini and then Via di Camollia to reach Porta di Camollia, the strongest and most dreaded gateway of Siena opened onto and concluded the Via Cassia, that came from Florence. The gateway we see today was rebuilt in 1604, to designs by Alessandro Casolani. According to historical sources, the stone decorations were carved by the sculptor Domenico Cafaggi. The external arch of Porta Camollia bears the famous inscription that was carved onto it to honor Ferdinand I de' Medici's arrival in Siena: COR MAGIS TIBI SENA PANDIT (Siena welcomes you with open arms) and that is now symbolic of the city's hospitality. Outside the Porta Camollia, we come to the Villa Seminario Regionale of Montarioso, that housed the **Museo Diocesano di Arte Sacra** (The Diocesan Museum of Sacred Art) of great historical and artistic interest. The museum is temporarily closed and will eventually be moved to the Ospedale di Santa Maria della Scala. One of the most outstanding pieces in the museum is the *Madonna of the Milk* by A. Lorenzetti.

The Salimbeni keep, with the nineteenth century façade by Partini; right: *the great hall of the keep (property of the Monte dei Paschi di Siena).*

The Life of the Virtuous Susanna, by Francesco Vanni (property of the Monte dei Paschi di S

PIAZZA DEI SALIMBENI

Returning to Via di Camollia and Via Montanini, we will come to Piazza Salimbeni. The piazza, as we see it today, was redesigned at the end of the XIX century by the purist architect Giuseppe Partini. Most of it, on the right side, was taken from the gardens of the Palazzo Spannocchi. The front was a long corridor with the **Palazzo della Dogana, Palazzo Tantucci** and finally the **Rocca dei Salimbeni** on the left. The rocca, or keep was one of the major fortified complexes of Medieval Siena. After the uprisings of 1264 and 1268 the keep was torn down and later rebuilt, but the Republic finally banished the Salimbeni family and confiscated their property in 1419. It was taken

Palazzo Spannocchi.

over the by city which established the Salt and grain tax offices there. After it was purchased by the Monte dei Paschi di Siena bank in 1866 for the sum of Lit. 60.743 the architect Giuseppe Partini was commissioned to remodel it. In the spirit of Gothic revival that was then in vogue he made extensive changes to what remained of the original structure, raising and adding new structures and wings in imitation Gothic style. *The monument to Sallustio Bandini* (1880) by Tito Sarocchi was then placed in the middle of the square. The current headquarters of the **Monte dei Paschi di Siena** - that were restored by the architect Pier Luigi Spadolini (1962-73) who succeeded in gracefully combining modern structures with the old walls,

consists of the following XIII century architectural elements: the *tower, the Fondaco dei Salimbeni*, the *Rocca*, and the *Palazzetto di Ranieri Salimbeni.* Along with the historic archives that contain much information about the economic history of Siena, the Rocca dei Salimbeni also contains many, extremely valuable artworks that the bank has collected over the years. It is thanks to the Monte dei Paschi di Siena that many masterpieces that had been scattered throughout Italy over the past three centuries are now being brought back to Siena, where they were created during the era of the Republic. The collection includes works by Pietro Lorenzetti, Sassetta, Giovanni di Paolo, Sano di Pietro, Beccafumi and many others.

PIAZZA DEI TOLOMEI

From Piazza Salimbeni, we take Via Banchi di Sopra to Piazza dei Tolomei. In middle of the square there is a column, surmounted by the *Sienese She-wolf,* by Domenico Arrighetti, called the "Cavedone" (1610). The piazza is named after the famous Sienese family, the most powerful after the Salimbeni, their longtime rivals for domination over the city; the Tolomei also disputed and claimed supremacy over the government itself. The piazza is dominated by the **Palazzo dei Tolome**i, that came into being after the Castellare of the Consorteria dei Tolomei (which

Palazzo Tolomei.

Church of San Cristoforo.

in 1290 included some 120 families) had been demolished. Notwithstanding the disastrous fire of 1277, the splendid building we see today is certainly one of the finest in Siena, and probably dates back to 1270, with its elegant, double mullioned windows and the great hall on the ground floor which was restructured between 1430 and 1444. Today it is headquarters of the Sienese branch of the **Cassa di Risparmio di Firenze**, and a number of sculptured fragments (*small capitals, lion-heads, the torso of a she-wolf*), that were found during the 1971 restoration works, are also displayed here. On the opposite side of the square is the **Church of San Cristoforo**, one of the oldest in Siena (XI-XII century), famed for having been the headquarters of the Greater Council of the Republic (Consiglio della Campana) in the XII and XIII centuries. Unfortunately, after the terrible 1798 earthquake, the church was shortened and was given its neoclassical façade, by Tommaso and Francesco Paccagnini (1800), with the two (1802) *statues* by Giuseppe Silini and the Tolomei *coat of arms*. Next to the church is a charming *little cloister*, probably built around the beginning of the XIII century, with brick columns and stone capitals, that was rebuilt to a large extent during the restorations done in 1921.

SAN FRANCESCO

Behind the church of San Cristoforo, along Via del Giglio, we come to Piazza San Francesco and the Church of San Francesco. Anonymous Sienese chroniclers mention 1228 as the year in which the first church dedicated to St. Francis was built on the hill of the Castellaccia di Ovile. The decoration of the rough stone façade (the neo-Gothic decorations we see today were done in the late XIX century) with black and white

Façade of the church of San Francesco.

marble stripes was started just before the end of the XIII century, interrupted after only half the façade had been covered and never completed. The church, on the other hand, was enlarged, because it was too small, in 1326. Only the façade and the right side of the old Romanesque church remain; the left side was demolished once the new left wall had been completed and joined to the roof. The presbytery was entirely

XIV century Portal by Francesco di Giorgio Martini.

reconstructed on powerful arches, that open onto a magnificent underground crypt built into the steep hillside. The new enlarged church was finished in 1475, but then, in 1482, the walls were raised to match the increased width of the renovated church. Francesco di Giorgio was almost certainly the architect entrusted with the latter project. The lovely main portal, in pure Sienese

The transept;
below: *Crucifixion*
by Pietro Lorenzetti.

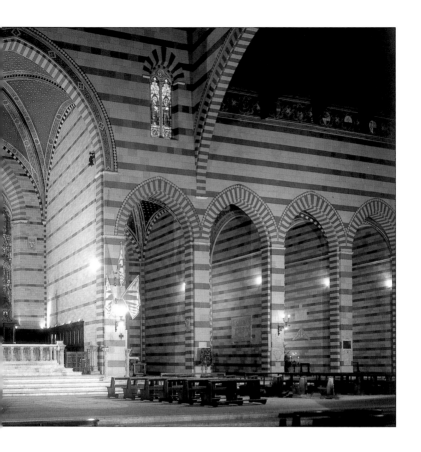

Renaissance style, is also worthy of his hand. After the façade was remodeled, the portal was moved inside the basilica, against the left wall where we can admire it today. The structural parts of the church that we see today were built by Francesco di Giorgio, but nearly all the treasures it used to contain were destroyed by the terrible fire of 25 August 1655, that even burned the marble and the altar. The few surviving paintings are now in the Pinacoteca Nazionale of Siena. In the (eighth) Bandini Piccolomini Chapel (dedicated to St. Bernardino), there are two great frescoes by Ambrogio Lorenzetti, portraying the *Martyrdom of Franciscan Friars* and *St. Louis of Toulose taking his leave from Pope Boniface VIII after abdicating his claim to the throne in favor of his brother Robert d'Anjou.* Notwithstanding their poor state of conservation, the frescoes still reveal Ambrogio's inventiveness and realism.

SANTA MARIA DI PROVENZANO

Returning from Piazza San Francesco along Via delle Vergini, we reach the Basilica of Santa Maria di Provenzano, in honor of whose much venerated image, the Palio race of 2 July is run. The Standard (Palio) is brought to the church before the race. On 2 July, it is taken to the Piazza del Campo and given to the winning Contrada, then, amidst a turmoil of rejoicing members of the victorious Contrada and of the allied or friendly Contrade, it is taken back to the Basilica, if only for a few minutes, to offer solemn thanks to the Virgin of Provenzano for the victory.

Construction of the basilica was started in 1595, and, architecturally speaking, was completed in 1604. It was consecrated on 16 October 1611. The design is based on the Roman church of Gesù, by Vignola, that best reflects the spirit of the Counter Reformation: a single, shortened nave, to facilitate preaching and a series of side altars, which, in this church, are simply set against the side walls and not surrounded by separate chapels as they are in the Roman church.

Church of Santa Maria di Provenzano.

Proceeding towards Via Banchi di Sotto, we will cross one of the most fascinating Medieval districts of Siena, which used to be where the great *castellari*, fortified mansions, used to stand. Next to the castellare of the Uguccioni family is the seat of the *University of* *Siena*, and facing it, the grandiose Palazzo Piccolomini, that houses the *State Archives*. It was begun around the middle of the XV century, by Bernardo Gambarelli, known as Rossellino, who brought the purest Florentine Renaissance civil architecture to Siena. Rossellino was the architect Pius II Piccolomini commissioned to build his model Renaissance jewel town of Pienza. The State Archives of Siena contain the famous and unique collection known as the **Museo delle tavolette della Biccherna**, that comprises 103 panel paintings and

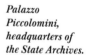

Palazzo Piccolomini, headquarters of the State Archives.

Annunciation among saints, by a Sienese artist (Jul./Dec. 1456), "Gabella" Panel. inv. nr. 30.

The Victory of Camollia, by Giovanni di Lorenzo Cini (post 1526),
"Gabella" Panel, inv. nr. 49.

only two painted canvases, that were the covers of the registers, which come from the Biccherna and Municipal Tax (Gabella del Comune), from the Ospedale di Santa Maria della Scala and from other Sienese administrative archives. Towards the middle of the XIII century the Biccherna (the main financial magistrature of Siena) adopted the practice of having the covers of the most important registers in its offices painted. The practice was also adopted by other financial magistratures and continued up to the XVIII century. The Biccherna collection constitutes a marvelously complete pictorial history of four centuries of Sienese life.

The interior of the synagogue.

SYNAGOGUE

The Jewish Temple of Siena, in the University district, was built in 1756, to neoclassical designs by the architect Giuseppe del Rosso. The wooden decorations were made by two master carpenters: Niccolò Ianda and Pietro Rossi. The *columns* flanking the Ark are supposed to have been made out of pieces of marble that came from Jerusalem and are particularly worthy of note. One of the finest surviving pieces of the original rich furnishing is the *circumcision throne* which was made in 1860. The Temple follows the Sephardic rite. Six curiously fashioned marble cavities have been recently discovered in the entrance hall. They are dated 1600 and were used for collecting offerings and contributions for the Jewish community of the time.

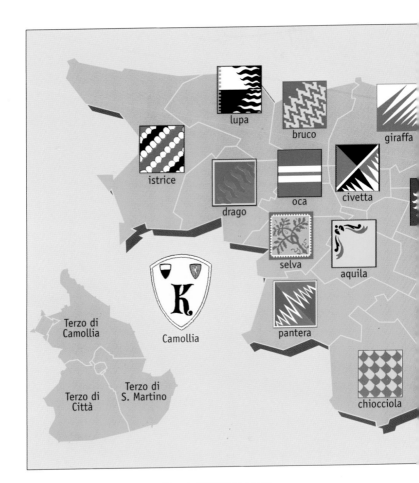

The map shows the following labeled districts and areas: lupa, bruco, giraffa, istrice, drago, oca, civetta, selva, aquila, Camollia, Terzo di Camollia, pantera, Terzo di Città, Terzo di S. Martino, chiocciola

THE CONTRADE
AND THE PALIO

by Antonio Zazzeroni

The Contrade (Districts) of Siena were created between the end of the XII and the beginning of the XIII century, and were responsible for administrative matters (tax collection, road maintenance) and public safety (police), etc. These institutions, that were based in the parish churches, that served both for public meetings and worship, were governed by a kind of mayor who was answerable directly to the Podestà (Chief of Justice) and was assisted by councilors elected by the people of the Contrada. The structure of the Contrade was completed after the formation of Compagnie Militari (the army of the Republic) in which every able man from 18 to 70 years of age had to serve. The Compagnie Militari were, in turn, grouped into the so-called "Terzi" (Thirds), cor-

San Martino

ocorno

nicchio

nda

valdimontone

a

Città

responding to the three territorial divisions or districts of the city: the Terzo di Citta (a white cross on red ground), the Terzo di San Martino (St. Martin and the beggar on a burgundy ground), and the Terzo di Camollia (a black K on white ground). Each Terzo was commanded by a Gonfaloniere Maestro, or standard-bearer. The Captain of the People bore a standard with a Crowned Lion Rampant on red ground: he was the supreme Commander of the Militia. In the XIV century, the clans of Siena were distributed among the 42 Contrade, which were reduced to 23 between the XV and XVI centuries. In time, the political and administrative reasons that had led to the creation of the Contrade, virtually disappeared and the latter turned their attention more and more to the organization of public games that long flourished in the town. The 23 Contrade took the names of *Aquila* (Eagle), *Bruco* (Caterpillar), *Chiocciola* (Snail), *Civetta* (Owl), *Drago* (Dragon), *Gallo* (Rooster), *Giraffa* (Giraffe), *Istrice* (Porcupine), *Leone* (Lion), *Liocomo or Leocorno* (Unicorn), *Liofante or Torre* (Elefant or Tower), *Lupa* (She-wolf), *Montone* (Ram), *Nicchio* (Shell), *Oca* (Goose), *Onda* (Wave), *Orso* (Bear), *Pantera* (Panther), *Quercia* (Oak), *Selvalta or Selva* (Forest), *Spadaforte* (Sword), *Tartuca* (Tortoise), and *Vipera* (Viper). No documentation exists explaining why the names (that were probably the fruit of popular imagination or related to some special event) were actually chosen. 1675 seems to be when six of these Contrade were suppressed, to wit: Gallo, Leone, Orso, Quercia, Spadaforte and Vipera.

THE CONTRADE TODAY

Today's Contrade are old institutions with a following that keeps growing year after year. The members are committed, insofar as possible, to carrying on their traditions and supporting them financially. (Each contradaiolo - contrada member- pays annual dues, called "protettorato") The organization of the contrade consists of decision-making and executive bodies that are established as needed. One of the most important sectors is dedicated to the young people who are the future of the contrade and the Palio. They are taught the history of the race, with specific emphasis on their respective contrade. The "Women's group" of each contrada generally deals with this issue almost exclusively. The women's group is also in charge of preparing parties for the little ones, on the feast of the Nativity of the Virgin, 8 September. The children decorate the shrine with the image of the Virgin Mary in the most typical part of the district and in the evening a street dinner is held just for them. The most solemn event, however, is the feast day of the patron saint of the contrada which is celebrated on the Sunday closest to the day. The streets are illuminated by the "braccialetti", carved wooden lamps, painted in the contrada's colors, holding bunches of light-bulbs and with old terra-cotta lamps filled with tallow and wick that burn through most of the night. On the eve of the feast, the Prior of the Contrada, accompanied by the Seggio (the governing body) and the Popolo (the people of the contrada) goes to the boundary of the district and meets the leaders of the allied contrade. Then, preceded by drums and standard-

bearers they go to the oratory for Vespers. At the end of the service the people pour back into the streets for the "children's palio", the "sack race", the "climbing the May-pole" and other games invented for the occasion. But, above all, they sing a song, that is common to all seventeen contrade; it is about Siena and is embellished with extem-

The rooftops of Siena.

poraneous rhymes either singing the praises of the contrada or ridiculing its rivals. Naturally, wine is served in abundance and the celebrations last late into the night. In the morning Mass is celebrated in the Oratory and the "Comparsa", consisting of dozens of participants, including drummers and standard-bearers winds its way through the city to pay tribute to the "protectors". The procession is repeated the following Sunday through streets outside the city walls, and is known as the "giro di campagna" or "country tour". In the evening the procession returns to the city, followed by the Prior, the Seggio and the Popolo.

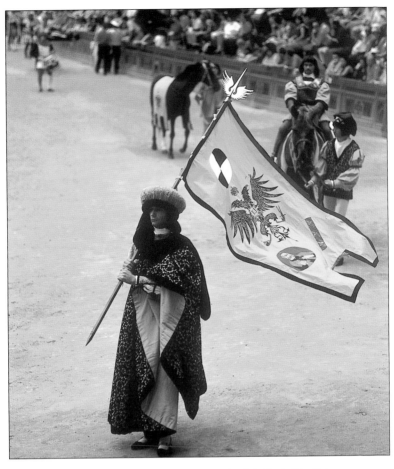

Poggio Maggiore of the Noble Contrada of the Eagle (Aquila).

THE SOCIETÀ DI CONTRADA

The "Società di Contrada" were established early in the XIX century to organize the contrada's yearly activities. These associations, with headquarters in premises adjacent to those of the contrada itself and that include rooms for meetings, dances and entertainment, game rooms, refreshment bar and a well-equipped kitchen are involved in many cultural, athletic and social-charity (such as the blood donors group) activities and programs. The bar and other services are managed by the contradaioli, who without pay or social distinctions take turns serving at the bar or waiting on tables. The kitchens are run mainly by the women's group that prepares the dinners and the banquet on the eve of the Palio (if the contrada is running that season), known as the Cena della Prova Generale, or Dress Rehearsal Dinner, for 1,000 or more guests.

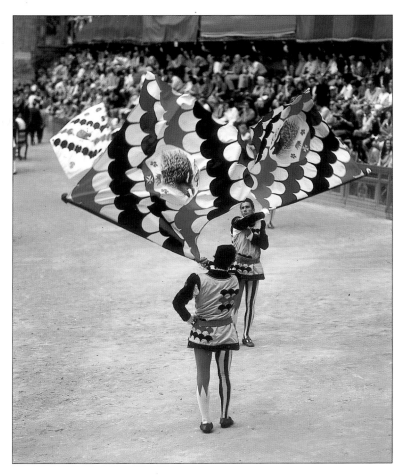

Standard bearers of the Contrada of the Porcupine (Istrice).

"DRAWING" THE CONTRADE

The first act of the Palio is the drawing: it is held about one month before the race (the last Sunday in May for the July palio and the Sunday after the July race for the August palio). Ten contrade take part in the Carriera or race. The rules governing the drawing are actually much less complex than they seem at first glance. The July race is run by the seven contrade that did not participate in the preceding July edition, and the other three are chosen, by lot, from amongst the contrade that had participated, thus giving each edition of the race the required 10 participating contrade. The same method is applied to the Palio held in August. Thus, the two "carriere", July and August are completely independent of each other insofar as the participating contrade are concerned. It may happen that a particularly lucky Contrada gets to participate in both races in one year, but that means that it will be automatically excluded from the races the following year, unless its name is drawn again. On the morning of the day of the drawing, the banners of the seven contrade that are participating by right are displayed on the first floor windows of the Palazzo Pubblico. In the afternoon, the other three participating contrade are drawn by lot; this is done by the mayor and the Captains. The flags of the three selected contrade are then displayed to tell the crowds, anxiously gathered outside the building which have been selected. The flags of the contrade that were not

Drummers, trumpeters, musicians and standard-bearers lead the Historical Pageant.

chosen are displayed from the upper floor, telling which ones will be automatically allowed to run in the following years' race. In the event of an extraordinary palio held for some special event, all ten contrade may run.

For a Sienese, the words "Terra in Piazza", literally earth on the Piazza del Campo, mean Palio: joy, hope and rivalry. The whole town is transformed and pulses with intense, unforgettable, almost magical life, especially if you have the opportunity to watch from the top of some tower in the evening. Shouts, laughter, and songs surge from street to street, from square to square, up to the final explosion (this time, only in the winning contrada) after the race. These are the moments of great joy to a Sienese, and can only be compared to the moment in which the Palio is handed down to the winning Contrada in the Piazza and to the other moment of totally pagan exultation that assails the people of the victorious Contrada when they pour into Santa Maria di Provenzano or into the Cathedral to offer thanksgiving for their victory. Several days before the race, the road around the Piazza is covered with a thick layer of earth, to make it easier for the horses to run. The stands for the spectators, the Judges' stand, where the Captains and Lieutenants of the

Contrade also sit, as well as the stand of the Priori are set up against the buildings around the square. The former near the Costarella dei Barbieri (the start and finish line), the latter near the Chiasso Largo. The concave center of the square, capable of holding some 40,000 spectators, is surrounded with metal barriers. At the Costarella dei Barbieri, a contraption, known as the "verrocchio" is set up. The "mossiere", the official and only starter uses this device that causes a thick rope, known as the "canapo" that is has been drawn taut across the track by a winch behind the barriers, to drop. A few meters behind this rope there is a shorter and thinner one stretched between the stands and the winch leaving just enough room for the horses to fit between the two ropes for the start of the race. A metal cage containing firecrackers that are set off at various moments during the race as signals is hoisted up next to the winch.

The "Tratta"
(Selecting the Horses)

Four days before the Palio (on 29 June for the July Palio and on 13 August for the Palio of the Assumption), the owners of the horses, (who must have veterinary certificates) lead their horses into the Podestà courtyard of the Palazzo Pubblico, early in the morning. The municipal officials identify the horses with a number called the "coscia" (flank) number, according to the order in which they are presented. A veterinarian, appointed by the City Council, checks the medical certificates and the horses' health. The horses are taken out, in groups of five or six at a time, ridden by the owners' jockeys or jockeys who ran in the Palio the year before. The horses have to circle the track three times (about 1000 meters in all). After the trials, three veterinarians very carefully check each horse and the Captains of the Contrade running in the Palio choose the ten horses that will run in the Palio. In the meantime, a large number of "contradaioli" usually gather in front of Palazzo Pubblico to watch the public assignment of the horses. The Mayor and the 10 Contrade Captains sit on a dais, set up in front of the Palazzo Public; there are also two urns on the dais. The 10 selected horses are led into horse boxes situated on the left of the platform. The Mayor puts 10 numbers (from 1 to 10) into one urn and the names of the 10 Contrade in the other. Two signboards hung above the dais, on the façade of the Palazzo Pubblico, will show which horse has been allotted to which Contrada. No substitutions are allowed after this time, if a horse falls sick or even dies before the race, the Contrada cannot replace its assigned steed. The "barbareschi" (grooms) who will lovingly care for their Contrada's horse up to the start of the race, wearing the colors of their respective Contrada, each take charge of the assigned horse, and lead it to the Contrada's stable.

THE TRIALS, THE PARTIES AND THE PALIO

As from the afternoon of the day of the "Tratta" the "barberi" (steeds) are taken for practice runs six times (morning and afternoon) before the race. They are rid-

The cart bearing the "Palio".

win the race, and they are not above using bribery. The negotiations continue in absolute secrecy right up to the last moment before the Palio. At last the day of days dawns. Early in the morning, the Archbishop of Siena celebrates Jockeys' Mass in the Cappella di Piazza, and the last trial, called the "provaccia" is run shortly afterwards. Then, the jockeys who will participate in the Palio are officially registered by the City Council. In the early afternoon, each Contrada church is crammed full of contrada members, while the co-rector blesses both horse and jockey and then, breaks the silence with the ritual words, "Go, and return victorious!". The "Comparse" of the Contrada, wearing their splendid costumes and waving their banners, start off for Piazza del Duomo, where the historical pageant forms up in front of the Prefecture. It also includes the representatives of the Sienese City Council, of the "guilds", of the University, of the City Councils of Massa Marittima and Montalcino, that took part in important events in Siena's history. Last of all comes the "Carroccio" the standard bearing cart, drawn by oxen and followed by a trumpeters and a mounted escort of knights from the noble Sienese families. The cart carries the "Balzana", Sienese Standard, and the Palio: a silk banner painted by famous Italian and foreign artists (traditionally the Palio for the July race is by a Sienese artist, while a famous artist from outside Siena creates the banner for the August race. The Palio, is given to the

den by the jockeys who are selected by the Contrade on the basis of the skill, experience and weight. The Captains and their Lieutenants spend these days getting the "partiti" (parties/allies) together, to scheme on how to damage the rival Contrade and above all how to winning Contrada, whereas the Contrada judged the best during the procession, both because of the stateliness of the Comparsa's behavior, as well as for the skills of the drummer and flag-wavers, will subsequently receive the *masgalano*, a finely chased silver plate. After accompanying their Comparsa to Piazza del Duomo, the people of the contrade take up their positions in piazza del Campo. Once the historical pageant has gone around the earth track on the Piazza del Campo, all the costumed representatives of the Contrade take their seats on the stand set up in front of the Palazzo Public. One drummer and one standard bearer for each Contrada stay on the track for final standard display, which is the last salute paid to the crowd before the race; in the meantime the Palio is hoisted into position on the Judges' Stand. And the race is on! At the signal, the horses, which are ridden bare-back by the jockeys, wearing the colors of the contrade and hard metal caps called "zucchini", are led out of the Courtyard of the Podestà. As they emerge, each jockey is given a "nerbo" or crop (made out of a dried bull's phallus) that can be used to urge on their own horses, or to hit the opposing horses or jockeys. They proceed to the "mossa", starting post where a special machine draws lots as to the order in which the horses are to enter the gap between the two ropes. As soon as the horse of the tenth and last Contrada enters the gap, the "mossiere" (starter) gives the

signal which will be repeated if he judges that the horses have gotten off to a false start. As soon as the rope drops, the horses spurt forward and the jockeys fight each other in every way they can. One of the horses will be the winner, even if he gets to the finish riderless, because it is the horse that gets to the end of the race that wins, not the rider. The deliriously exultant contrada members brandish their banners as the Palio is handed down to them from the judges' stand and chant their way towards the Victory Banquet. And the night will resound to their songs of joy. Torches will burn brightly from the Mangia tower, while the colors of the winning contrada hang triumphantly outside the triple mullioned window of the Palace.

THE VICTORIOUS CONTRADA CELEBRATES THE PALIO

The Contrade that have won the two Palio races of the year, generally organize two great banquets, a few days apart, in the month of September. The contrada is decked with flags and lights and trestle tables are set up along the streets, for the some 3-4000 hungry participants at the Victory Banquet. The Prior of the Contrada, flanked by the Captain and the victorious jockey will be given the places of honor, together with the officials and specially invited guests. Most important of all, in the center, opposite the places of honor, a small paddock with a manger, will be set up for the real winner, the horse. A journal entitled *Numero Unico* published by the contrada recounts the story of the race and its protagonists through pictures and articles.

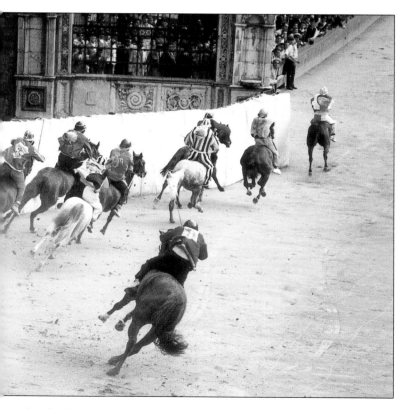

A breathtaking moment during the race.

USEFUL INFORMATION

EMERGENCY NUMBERS

Police Emergency ☎113

Carabinier ☎112

Ambulance ☎118

Fire Department ☎115

Questura - Police Headquarters
Via del Castoro ☎0577201111
Foreigners' Office
Piazza Jacopo della Quercia

Tax Department ☎117

**Government
Forestry Service** ☎1515

Emergency Road Service ☎116

**Telefono azzurro - Abused
Children's Hotline** ☎19696

INFORMATION

**APT - Tourist Bureau
Siena**
Piazza del Campo, 56 ☎0577280551
telefax 0577270676

**Italian State Railways
Information** ☎0577280115

HOTEL
RESERVATIONS

Piazza San Domenico ☎0577288084
telefax 0577280290

Protofur - Via Fontanella, 4
Parcheggio il Campo ☎057745900
telefax 0577283145

Associazione Albergatori Senesi
c/o Hotel Moderno
Via Baldassarre Peruzzi, 19
☎057747669

Terranostra
Federazione Provinciale Coltivatori
Diretti - Via Montanini, 63
☎057746006

Turismo Verde
Sede Provinciale Confederazione
Italiana Agricoltori - Via dei Termini, 6
☎057747157

Confcommercio
Sede Provinciale di Siena
Via dei Termini, 32 ☎0577248811

Confesercenti
Federazione Provinciale di Siena
Viale Toselli, 74 ☎0577252226

Unione Nazionale Consumatori
c/o ACLI La Lizza, 2 ☎0577281232

TRAVEL AGENCIES

Agenzia Viaggi Seti
Piazza del Campo, 56
☎0577228245
telefax 0577270676

BUS SERVICES

TRA-IN – City Lines
Tickets and Information
Piazza Gramsci ☎0577204246

TRA-IN – Intercity Lines
Tickets and Information
Piazza San Domenico ☎0577204245

TAXIS

Piazza Matteotti ☎0577289350
Piazza Stazione ☎057744504
Radio-taxi ☎057749222

CAR RENTAL

Balzana Autonoleggi
Via P. Fracassi, 2
☎0577285013 – 057746443

Giamello Giorgio
Via Guido da Siena, 7   ☎057750381

Periccioli Vasco
Via Principale, 19
Taverne d'Arbia   ☎0577364812

Sampieri Lorenzo
Strada S.S.73 Ponenete 142
☎0577394058

AVIS
De Martino Autonoleggi
Via Simone Martini, 36
☎0577270305 – 057749275

Hertz
Bellucci Daniele   ☎057745085

General Cars
Viale Toselli 20/26   ☎057740518
telefax 057747984

Minucci Benito
Viale Sardegna, 11   ☎0577282000

BUS CHARTER

Sena S.r.l.
Via Montanini, 92   ☎0577283203

BICYCLE RENTAL

DF Bike
Via Massetana Romana, 54
☎0577271905

Automotocicli Perozzi
Via del Romitorio, 5   ☎0577223157

A.C.I. Automobil Club d'Italia
Viale Vittorio Veneto, 47
☎057749001

HOTELS

Athena ★★★★
Via P. Mascagni, 55   ☎0577286313
telefax 057748153

Certosa di Maggiano ★★★★
Via di Certosa, 82   ☎0577288180
telefax 0577288189

Executive ★★★★
Via N. Orlandi, 32   ☎0577333173
telefax 0577333178

Garden
(Dipendenza) ★★★★
Via Custoza, 2   ☎057747056
telefax 057746050

Jolly Hotel Excelsior ★★★★
Piazza La Lizza, 1   ☎0577288448
telefax 057741272

Park Hotel ★★★★
Via Marciano, 18   ☎057744803
telefax 057749020

Villa Patrizia ★★★★
Via Fiorentina, 58   ☎057750431
telefax 057750431

Villaggio Albergo
Villa Scacciapensieri ★★★★
Via di Scacciapensieri, 10
☎057741441
telefax 0577270854

Academy ★★★
Via Lombardi   ☎0577332400
telefax 0577332409

Ai Tufi ★★★
Via Massetana Romana, 68
☎0577283292
telefax 0577284076

Arcobaleno ★★★
Via Fiorentina, 32-40   ☎0577271092
telefax 0577271423

Chiusarelli ★★★
Viale Curtatone, 15 ☎0577280562
telefax 0577271177

Garden ★★★
Via Custoza, 2 ☎057747056
telefax 057746050

Minerva ★★★
Via Garibaldi, 72 ☎0577284474
telefax 0577284474

Pensione Palazzo Ravizza ★★★
Pian dei Mantellini, 34☎0577280462
telefax 0577221597

Santa Caterina ★★★
Via E.S. Piccolomini, 35
☎0577283930
telefax 0577271087

Villa Liberty ★★★
Viale V. Veneto, 11 ☎057744966
telefax 057744770

Alex ★★
Via G. Gigli, 5 ☎0577282338

Il Giardino ★★
Via B. Peruzzi, 35 ☎0577285290
telefax 0577221197

Piccolo Hotel Il Palio ★★
Piazza del Sale, 19 ☎0577281131
telefax 0577281142

Piccolo Hotel Etruria ★★
Via delle Donzelle, 3 ☎0577288088
telefax 0577288461

Locanda Garibaldi ★
Via Giovanni Dupré, 18
☎0577284204

RESIDENCES

Casa Nuova 1° Cat.
Via R. Bianchi Bandinelli, 14
☎ e telefax 0577223170

Le Tolfe 1° Cat.
Strada delle Tolfe, 12 ☎057744322
telefax 057744591

Vico Alto 1° Cat.
Via R. Bianchi Bandinelli, 14
☎ e telefax 0577332460

Residence Le Grondaie 2° Cat.
Via delle Grondaie, 14
☎057744565
telefax 0577223540

Masotti Orio 3° Cat.
Via Alessandro VII, 3
☎0577288439
telefax 057756093

VACATION HOMES AND APARTMENTS

Le Meridiane 2° Cat.
Via P. Fracassi, 3 ☎0577280000

Villa Agostoli 2° e 3° Cat.
Strada degli Agostoli, 81 ☎057747056

Good Way 3° Cat.
Viale Vittorio Emanuele II, 50
☎ 0577270202

Colonna S. Marco 3° e 4° Cat.
Strada di Pescaia, 73 - ☎ 0578748501

CAMPSITES

Siena Colleverde ★★★
Strada di Scacciapensieri, 47
Aperto: 21/3 – 10/11 ☎0577280044
telefax 0577333298

HOSTELS

Guidoriccio
Via Fiorentina, Località Stellino
☎057752212
telefax 057756172

AGRITOURISM

Azienda Agraria Emma e Settimia
Str. S.73 Levante, 49-51 ☎0577364939

Fattoria Mociano
Loc. Taverne d'Arbia
☎e telefax 0577364815

Fattoria Il Ferraiolo
Strada di Montechiaro, 54
☎0577363013

I Pianali
Strada di Lecceto, 1 ☎0577314516

Il Poderaccio
Strada del Castagno, 1 ☎057753292

La Selva
Pian del Lago, 188 ☎0577318559
telefax 0577318656

Montalbuccio
Strada di Montalbuccio, 124
☎057742517

Villa Agostoli srl
Strada degli Agostoli, 81 ☎057747056

ROOMING HOUSES

1st Category

Formisano Lucia
Via del Paradiso, 21 ☎0577322508

Guidotti Catia
Str. Di Marciano, 46
☎ 057752511/057750355/0577282270

2nd Category

Bagnai Luigi
Via del Porrione, 91 ☎057740106

Bassi Lanfranco
Via del Paradiso, 54 ☎0577281458

Bisogno Angelina
Via dei Pispini, 144 ☎0577330125

Casoni Silvana
Vicolo della Tartuca, 1 ☎057750945

Checcacci Maria Grazia
Viale Cavour, 76 ☎0577281458

Del Bravo Alessandro
Via Paolo Mascagni, 2/4 ☎0577285193

Grazzini Giulio
Via Garibaldi, 70 ☎0577378282

Maffei Ernesto
Via del Porrione, 77 ☎0577222713

Massi Clementina
Via Pantaneto, 162 ☎0577284434

Taddei Aida
Via Enrico Fermi, 18/20 ☎057745008

3rd Category

Ardenghi Marina
Via Cecco Angiolieri, 36 ☎057754347

Bini Mauro
Via Stalloreggi, 48 ☎057743439

Carli Maria
Via Celso Cittadini,17 ☎0577288395

Ferrara Giovanna
Via Pantaneto, 125 ☎0577223815

Gragnoli Alma
Via G. Tommasi, 4 ☎057750945

Niccolini Andrea
V.le V. Emanuele II,1 ☎0577284204

Seminara Anna Maria
Via Cassia Sud, 248 ☎0577378048

Terzuoli Renata
Via Vallerozzi, 106 ☎057740681

Vagaggini Patrizia
Via dei Rossi, 77 ☎057743041

4rd Category

Caini Vasco
Via S. Caterina, 10 ☎0577287805

Fornacelli Laura
Via dei Termini, 13 ☎057747955

Leonini Oretta
Via Sallustio Bandini, 39 ☎0577284474

Longo Domenico
Via dei Gazzani, 6
☎ e fax 0577289364

Ridolfi Lorena
Via Quinto Settano, 29 ☎057741184

Sensi Silvano
Via Camollia, 128 ☎0577285120

MUSEUMS AND GALLERIES

Palazzo Comunale
Piazza del Campo ☎0577292263

Torre del Mangia
Piazza del Campo ☎0577292342

Spedale Santa Maria della Scala
Piazza Duomo ☎0577224828

Pinacoteca Nazionale
Palazzo Buonsignori
Via San Pietro, 29 ☎0577281161

Duomo Piazza del Duomo

Libreria Piccolomini in Duomo
Museo dell'Opera Metropolitana
Piazza del Duomo ☎057742309

Battistero di San Giovanni
Piazza San Giovanni ☎057742309

Oratorio di San Bernardino
Piazza San Francesco

Museo Archeologico Nazionale
Spedale Santa Maria della Scala
Piazza Duomo ☎0577224828

Archivio di Stato
Palazzo Piccolomini
Banchi di Sotto, 52 ☎057741271

Biblioteca Comunale degli Intronati
Via della Sapienza, 5 ☎0577280704/5

Santuario e Casa di Santa Caterina
Costa di S. Antonio ☎057744177

Museo della Società Esecutori Pie Disposizioni in Siena
Via Roma, 71 ☎0577284300

Museo Bologna Buonsignori
Via Roma, 50 ☎0577284300

Oratorio della Società Esecutori Pie Disposizioni
Piazza Duomo, 1 ☎0577284300

Orto Botanico
Via Pier Andrea Mattioli, 4
☎0577298874

Musei di Storia Naturale
Accademia dei Fisiocritici
Prato di S. Agostino, 5 ☎057747002

Museo Aurelio Castelli
Basilica dell'Osservanza
☎0577332444

Osservatorio di Poggio al Vento
Osservatorio Sismico, Meteorologico, Astronomico
Strada dei Cappuccini, 100
☎057744336

Enoteca Italiana
Fortezza Medicea
☎0577288497 fax 0577270717

Contrada Museums

Aquila
Casato di Sotto   ☎0577288086

Bruco
Via del Comune, 44   ☎057744842

Chiocciola
Via San Marco, 37   ☎057745455

Civetta
Piazzetta del Castellare ☎0577285505

Drago
Piazza Matteotti, 19   ☎057740575

Giraffa
Via delle Vergini, 18   ☎0577287091

Istrice
Via Camollia, 87
               ☎057748495/057743330

Leocorno
Via di Follonica, 15   ☎057749298

Lupa Via Vallerozzi, 71/73
               ☎0577270777

Nicchio
Via dei Pispini, 68   ☎057749600

Oca
Vicolo del Tiratoio, 11
               ☎0577285413-0577282534

Onda Via Giovanni Dupré, 111
               ☎057748384

Pantera
Via San Quirico
               ☎057748468-0577289055

Selva
Piazzetta della Selva   ☎057745093

Tartuca
Via T. Pendola, 21   ☎057749448
Torre
Via Salicotto, 76
               ☎0577222181-0577222555

Valdimontone
Via di Valdimontone, 6
               ☎0577222590-057749896

Sport facilities

"A. Franchi" Municipal Stadium
               ☎0577281084

Athletic Field
Viale Avignone   ☎057744955

Athletic Field
Loc. Acqua Calda   ☎057751505

Municipal Swimming Pool
Piazza G. Amendola   ☎057747496

Municipal Swimming Pool
Loc. Acqua Calda   ☎057752667

University Sports Center
Via L. Banchi, 3   ☎057754114

La Racchetta - Tennis Club
Via Vivaldi, 2   ☎0577221110

Circolo Tennis Siena - Tennis Club
Strada di Vico Alto   ☎0577333464

Tennis Campansi - Tennis Club
Via Campansi, 18   ☎0577270560

Riding - Club Ippico Senese
Loc. Pian del Lago   ☎0577318677

Costone
Via del Costone, 9   ☎057742073

Dopolavoro Ferroviario Siena
Piazza Rosselli, 19   ☎057744501

Etrusca Corse Cavalli srl
Loc. Pian delle Fornaci
               ☎0577394347–0577393497
Mens Sana
Palazzetto dello Sport Viale A. Sclavo
               ☎057747298

Target Shooting
Str. Di Peragna, Torre Fiorentina
               ☎057752417

Virtus Via Vivaldi   ☎0577221055

Restaurants

Ai Tre Cristi – Via Provenzano, 1/7
               ☎0577280608

Al Mangia
Piazza del Campo, 42   ☎0577281121

Al Marsili
Via del Castoro, 3   ☎057747154

Antica Trattoria Botteganova
Via Chiantigiana, 29   ☎0577284230

Da Enzo
Via Camollia, 49   ☎0577281277

Grotta del Gallo Nero
Via del Porrione, 67   ☎0577284356

Grotta di Santa Caterina
Via della Galluzza, 24 ☎0577282208

Il Campo
Piazza del Campo, 50   ☎0577280725

Il Mestolo
Via Fiorentina, 85   ☎057751531

La Taverna di Cecco
Via C. Angiolieri, 19   ☎0577288518

TRATTORIAS

Antica Trattoria Papei
Piazza del Mercato, 6 ☎0577280894

Camollia
Via Camollia, 130   ☎057747506

Da Dino
Casato di Sopra, 71   ☎0577289036

Ezio
Viale Vitt.Emanuele II,32
                        ☎ 057748094

Guidoriccio
Via Dupré, 18   ☎057744350

La Taverna di Bacco
Via di Beccheria, 9   ☎057749331

La Vecchia Osteria
Via S. Marco, 8   ☎0577287133

L'Osteria
Via dei Rossi, 79   ☎0577287592

Osteria Buca di S. Pietro
Vicolo di S. Pietro, 4   ☎057740139

Osteria Il Tamburino
Via Stalloreggi, 11   ☎0577280306

PIZZERIAS
AND
TAKE-AWAYS

Bistrot
Via del Rialto, 4   ☎057747243

Costa
Piazza del Campo, 37 ☎0577280614

Il Cavallino Bianco
Via di Città, 20   ☎057744258

La Fortezza Via Cesare Battisti, 8
                        ☎057748095

Lo Spiedo
Via Camollia, 23   ☎057742260

Osteria del Coro
Via Pantaneto, 85   ☎0577222482

Pizzeria La Colonna
Strada Massetana, 58   ☎057740469

Pizzeria S. Marco
Pian dei Mantellini, 46 ☎057742277

CINEMAS

Cineforum
Piazza dell'Abbadia, 6
☎0577283044
Fiamma
Via Pantaneto, 141   ☎0577284503
Impero
V.le V. Emanuele II, 14 ☎057748260
Metropolitan
Piazza G. Matteotti   ☎057747109
Moderno
Via di Calzoleria   ☎0577289201
Nuovo Pendola
Via S. Quirico, 13   ☎057743012
Odeon
Banchi di Sopra, 31   ☎057742976

CLUBS AND DISCOS

Al Cambio
Via Pantaneto, 48 ☎057743183
Barone Rosso
Via dei Termini, 9
Caffè 115
Via dei Rossi, 115
Gallery
Via Pantaneto, 13 ☎0577285310
L'Officina
Piazza del Sale, 3 ☎0577286301

HOTELS
OUTSIDE SIENA

CASOLE D'ELSA
Gemini★★★★
Strada Provinciale, 4 ☎0577948622
telefax 0577948241
Pietralata★★★
Via del Teschio, 35 ☎0577948657
telefax 0577948468

CASTELLINA IN CHIANTI
Fattoria Casafrassi★★★★
Strada Chiantigiana ☎0577740621
telefax 0577740805
Belvedere di San Leonino★★★
Loc. San Leonino, 23 ☎0577740887
telefax 0577740924
Locanda Le Piazze★★★
Loc. Le Piazze ☎0577743190
telefax 0577743191

CHIUSDINO
Il Palazzetto★★
Fraz. Palazzetto, 60/62 ☎0577751160
telefax 0577751160

COLLE VAL D'ELSA
Arnolfo★★★
Via F. Campana, 8 ☎0577922020
telefax 0577922324
Villa Belvedere★★★
Loc. Belvedere, via Senese ☎0577920966
telefax 0577924128

GAIOLE IN CHIANTI
Castello di Spaltenna★★★
Loc. Spaltenna, 13 ☎0577749483

Residence San Sano★★★
Strada Chiantigiana, 29 ☎0577746130
telefax 0577746156

MONTALCINO
Bellaria★★★
Via Osticcio, 19 ☎0577848668

Dei Capitani★★★
Via Lapini, 6 ☎0577847227
telefax 0577847238

MONTERIGGIONI
Hotel Monteriggioni★★★★
Via 1° Maggio, 4 ☎0577305009
telefax 0577305011
Anna★★★
S.S.222 - Loc. Fontebecci ☎057751371
telefax 057751371

RADDA IN CHIANTI
Relais Fattoria Vignale★★★★
Via Pianigiani, 8 ☎0577738300
telefax 0577738592

Vescine★★★
Loc. Vescine ☎0577741144
telefax 0577740263

RADICONDOLI
Giogliano★★★
Loc. Giogliano ☎0577790563

La Sorgente★★★
Loc.Bagni delle Galleraie ☎0577793150

RAPOLANO TERME
Grand Motel Serre★★★★
Loc. Crocevie ☎0577704777
telefax 0577704780
Terme di San Giovanni★★★
Loc.Terme di S.Giovanni ☎0577724030
telefax 0577724053

SAN QUIRICO D'ORCIA
Le Terme★★★
Bagno Vignoni ☎0577887150
telefax 0577887497
Palazzuolo★★★
Via S.Caterina, 43 ☎0577897080
telefax 0577898264

INDEX